the party at limbo peak

NEW ITERATIONS OF THE DISCORDIAN FRACTAL

Several animals were eaten during the making of this book. They were delicious.

After you read this book, it will be in your head.

When you want to create something, you can use just about anything which is inside your head. Unfortunately, some people believe that ideas are like objects - they think you can own them, and through that ownership, control them.

In a legal sense, this is true. Mickey Mouse is featured prominently in my childhood memories, but I do not have the freedom to draw upon those personal experiences in certain ways. I am not legally allowed to create a new story about Mickey. If I draw him, I can't sell it or hang it up in a classroom. Part of my imagination belongs to Disney.

In contrast, we are not guarding the information in this book. Unlike Disney, we accept that we lose control of an idea as soon as it passes our lips. This book is yours. You may photocopy it to your heart's content. You may cut out the pages and rearrange them. You may write new stuff based on what you've read here. You can chuck it in a fire for all we care. We call it KopyLeft: All Rites Reversed.

Malaclypse the Younger and Omar Khayyam Ravenhurst made their own holy book, called the Principia Discordia. They filled it with words and images that resonated with them. Old ideas were juxtaposed in a way which created new meaning. They invited all of us to the party. This is the Strange Times and everybody gets to write their own Bible for a change. Even spags like you.

It's your head, after all. Do what you want with it.

ISBN 978-0-557-71885-6

WE'D LIKE TO THANK THE CONTRIBUTORS BELOW, AS WELL AS THE CONTRIBUTORS WE FORGOT TO LIST BELOW:

Baron von Hoopla ♔ Cain ♔ Cainad ♔ Cramulus ♔ Dirtyessence ♔ Ed Wilson ♔ Enrico Salazar ♔ Full Time Slacker ♔ Golden Applesauce ♔ Ignatious Dryroasted Chaffinch ♔ LHX ♔ LMNO ♔ Malaclypse the Tertiary ♔ Mangrove ♔ Nigel ♔ P3nt4gr4m ♔ Payne ♔ Princess Madnonymus ♔ Princess Unicornia ♔ Ratatosk ♔ Rev.-What's-His-Name ♔ Reverend Loveshade ♔ Richter ♔ Scott Lynn Hamilton ♔ Sepia ♔ 5hroom Bob Penta Pantz ♔ The Good Reverend Roger (whose rotting carcass is stuffed under Joe Arpaio's floorboards) ♔ the Outer Myspace Discordians ♔ Undue ♔ Vexati0n ♔ Wes Unruh ♔ William S. Burroughs ♔ Zarathud's prehensile anus

FUCK WHAT YOU THINK YOU KNOW ABOUT CHAOS

Table of Contents

May 27th - June 2nd / Confusion 1st - Confusion 7th
YOU are invited to the
Discordian CYBERSPACE MASQUERADE
Shed your old internet identity. Come in "disguise". Rub elbows with Discordians and kin from all over the net. Swap ideas. Have new ones. Find the others.
HAIL ERIS
JOIN THE PARTY http://we.dontexist.net

Introduction

The Gods were annoyed
To say the least.

But they had no choice 'cause we had rented the space fair and square. The ink on the contract was dry. The Gods' job was to clear out and spend the week on an all-expenses-paid booze cruise through the Astral. Our job was to use their space to party like it's 2012. Apollo, in his little white vacation shoes, flipped me off on the way out. They had just heard the news, that Limbo Peak had been rented out by *Discordians.*

When Triple Zero and I reserved the place, we wore these sweet masks. I was Hairacles and he was Kolonoskopos. We told them it was a masquerade ball, but we didn't tell 'em who was on the guest list.

When Zeus found out it was Discordians, he got all bitchtits. "Eris worshippers?" he thundered. "Aw Hera, *they're gonna foul the pool...*" Someone whispered in his ear that skinnydipping was listed *several times* on the party agenda. That old windbag's bitchtits practically burst out his beardhole. "I forbid the pool entirely!" Sure thing pops. Yeah, we'll be good guests. Hey, where do you keep the towels?

Our Lady Eris is celebrating 49 or 50 years or so since she sent her chimpanzee to freak out those spags Mal and Omar. It's been more or less a constant party since then - like something Crowley would envision while balls deep in an ass trance. In a way we're celebrating 49 or 50 years of constant partying with an even *weirder* party.

So 000 and I -- I mean, Hairacles and Kolonoskopos -- tried to contact as many "Discordians" as they could find for this bizarre masquerade bash. Weird people in their anybody suits. We're all over the place like tossed cookies. And when the party started, they came in droves. They jibbered in Russian. There were mittens and win in every discussion.

Now there's a lot of "Discordians" out there on the web, and obviously they're not organized really well, so there's no telling how much of the iceberg we crashed. But I think we got a good sampling. It was cool, because all these foreign networks collided. They swapped ideas and peed in the idea pot. And this book is the toxic soup that we squeezed out of it.

The idea, originally, was to produce a book *really quickly*. I had this idea for a booklet I wanted to write about why *Discordia* is actually pretty useful in dealing with this crazy decade. The Principia Discordia is practically 50 years old, but it keeps getting more relevant. Every day, my commute to work feels more like a stanza from Lewis Carroll. I think the Principia is a better guide to navigating the Madness than any of the other models stuck to my shoe like toilet paper. So I put together some of my thoughts, but I wanted more people to give their spin on things. So I had this idea for a shortlived one-shot internet forum.

To make a long story short, we set up the Internet Cyberspace Masquerade (also known as the Party at Limbo Peak). We got as many people as we could to put on made-up-identity masks and show up at this forum. It would only be open for one week, so there was no time for a culture to form. No time for in-group/out-group follow the leader in-joke/bad-joke memetics. Separated from their networks and social backup, people were forced to talk straight. It was an interesting experiment.

And that's the energy which launched this book: A bunch of random factors coming together to form a social collage. I think that's a good thumbnail of the Discordian society right there - there are artists, hackers, occultists, pranksters, the remnants of Norton's Empire. They're surrealist tricksters who live on the fringes, colorful iterations at the edge of the fractal. They've got all these great ideas, but those ideas are scattered all over the board. I say let's cut 'em up into kibble and assemble them, collage style, into a ransom note to reality. Let's make a primordial stone soup.

And since the Masquerade, the book has continued to grow. If anything, I want it to stand as a signpost, reminding future generations that though many of our forefathers have fallen (rest in pieces Greg, Kerry, Bob et al), we're still here. We're still *doing stuff.* Are you?

This book is about some of the energy going on right now. It's a rough sketch of the view from Limbo Peak. It's not the whole enchilada. It's like trying to get a sense of what a party was like by listening to a tape recording of it. Only a snippet. This book is a cutup, a collage, just like you. Take the parts of it you like. Rip out the rest.

The PDF for this book is free and kopyleft. That means you can make it yours. If you don't like some of the stuff here, just tear it out. Print out your favorite pages, add your own. Sell 'em for all I care. Make cutups. Make millions. Pull it out and make it happen.

Like a woman trying on a hundred dresses, the writings in this book love sexy new juxtapositions. They'd love to sneak into mailboxes, be stapled to trees, and handed to strangers. They like how the symbols on the page nuzzle the symbols in one's head. They like how those heads nuzzle each other. It's like a big freakin' nuzzlefest from cover to cover.

For those of you who are reading this but have no idea what this *Discordia* thing is, maybe I should offer some brief, half-assed explanation. Discordia "is" a religion in some sense, a philosophy in some sense, a joke in some sense, a bunch of jerks in some sense and a recipe for disaster in some sense. What these five senses have in common is Chaos. The name at the center of the hurricane is Eris, the Greek Goddess of strife and confusion. She doesn't take much seriously these days. We think it's best to laugh.

Contemporary Discordia first appeared in 1958 or 1959 (depending on which part of the *Principia Discordia* you're forbidden to believe). Discordians have infiltrated all parts of culture from summer blockbusters to the Planet Eris. They appreciate Chaos, which they see as a balancing act between Order and Disorder. They (read: you) think that society is too "serious business" right now (right?), and are pursuing a million and one ways to DO something about it. I don't want to say too much because Discordia involves some very personal revelations and I don't want to spoil the surprise. So read up on it. The symbols in your head will reflect off the symbols you read and give you a brand new correct interpretation of Grand and Glory Old Discordja gift wrapped with your own nervous system. We're tricksters, and the person we want you to trick is yourself. Discordians observe no rules except those they make for themselves. This is actually true for every man, woman, child, and cabbage on this earth but barely any of them realize that. The Pope of Discordia (read: you) can grant you permission to do whatever the hell you want. So kiss his ass. Or kick it. It's up to you.

Zarathud tugged at my leg. "Look at that," he said, pointing to the ceiling. Above the front door, someone had painted big bright red letters which spelled out the word GOAT. What? Why did someone write GOAT on the ceiling? I never resolved this question, and it itched my brain like madness. For weeks afterwards, I would look up every time I entered a building.

IT WAS LIKE A COMPULSION -- I COULDN'T GO THROUGH A DOOR WITHOUT LOOKING FOR THE ABSURD.

St. Bacon Cone Nixon has another approach. She likes pranks that the victim might not even notice. "I like to plant products in people's houses. I'll replace their half-used jug of milk with a half-used jug of different milk, or put a handful of mayonnaise packets in their butter compartment. It's subtle enough to make them question their own realities. You can add magazines to their bedside table or stuff a pair of socks under the blanket at the foot of the bed. Maybe try adding a pair of shoes in their size to their closet. I prefer things which really do fuck with people's *minds*, making it a *mind*fuck and not just an irritating obvious prank."

But sometimes it can be blaringly obvious. Like putting your e-mail address on a crazy poster and hang it out to cool. You'll attract the sort of people that send e-mails to people who put up crazy signs. (I've met them, they're good people) I've been leaving weird stuff on the train for years, and now I'm starting to see weird stuff that I didn't even do. People have been cutting up the ads and reassembling them into surreal art. Now the train is a canvas. Brilliant stuff like this makes me want to explode into a flock of birds all singing.

Have you heard of the Retail Cabal? It's every interesting person that works a boring retail job and made it into a living shrine to Our Lady Discord. When I worked for Lord Tayloron, I dedicated myself to writing FNORD on every single bill I could get my hands on. (FNORD YOUR ONES!) At a critical moment in an unrelated story, I'd get a FNORDed five-dollar bill as change. The handwriting was foreign, and there was no moustache on Washington, so it clearly wasn't mine. If you love your weirdness, let it go. It'll come back fivefold.

This is the energy which prompted Synaptaclypse Generator (the guy who operates poee.co.uk) to start the annual *Day of Discord* - August 23rd, when Discordians are encouraged to go out of their way to meet and beat each other. Us spags got together and we went a-postering in White Plains NY, then got pancakes. When we returned to my car, someone had put a big-ass poster on the windshield saying that they loved our posters and they wanted to hang out with us. An e-mail address was included. So even if they don't know it yet, our people are out there. Way out there. So put your weird out there like weirdbait. Let it hang out of your spaggy pants. These things are signposts to the Others.

And this book is a signpost too, a signal flare, like secret hobo code. We're here, we're real, and you can be a real one too.

Zarathud, it turns out, is a big fan of the cut-up method. You'll notice he wandered through the book and made his own edits. He's had a lot of fun rearranging stuff and making it "better". He approached me at the party and said, "Hey, can I be in the book?"

"Sure," I said, toweling off the ostrich.

He told me he was worried that since he's the Apostle of the fourth season, Bureaucracy, people think he's a total square. Well it's true that he's not very creative, and his sense of humor can be a bit morbid, but he's got quite the knack for odd juxtapositions. For the Apostle of Laws and Red Tape, he sure loves to use his scissors.

For example, I had two essays I wanted to show you about cutups and collages. One from this book, The Art of Memetics, and one by old man William Burroughs. Zarathud liked the pieces, so during his lunch break at the Jade Emperor's Bureaucratorium, (it's in the food court of Chinese Heaven) he shuffled them together. Now I can't tell if we're reading Burroughs writing about memetics or Ed and Wes writing about cutups, but Zarathud tells me that he's taking credit personally for the "new" piece.

Credit? I hadn't even thought of that. If anything, we want to avoid notice. Zeus is pissed that we jumped on the beds and skinny dipped in the hot tub and my ass was all over the kitchen counter. And if mythology has taught me anything, you do not want Greek Gods all bitchtits at you.

After all, Eris hasn't gone anywhere but crazy. Discordia, this weird neophilic irreligion, this bastard daughter of agnosticism and paganism and satire and flax, only ends in delirium and strife. If anything, this book should stand as a sign post saying "DANGER". It's an old crone, poised at the edge of Madness and Nothingness, crying "Go away! This place is cursed! Cursed I tell you, beware!" So turn back now. Save yourself from this postmodern nightmare: the ramblings of a nonexistent society which thrives in a nonexistent place in the umbra of the 21st century. THROW OUT your heretical humor and remove that troublemaker tongue from your cheek. Don't you know that people worked really hard to create this straightjacket civilization? There's centuries of work poured into these illusions. Don't you know that the real world is cold and and you've gotta steel yourself to meet it? Armor your heart with ice and nothing will harm you ever again. Work is sacred. Laughter is for children. Grow UP already, grow UP.

Jeez, I can't even write that trash with a straight face. This is part of what the Discordian Fractal looks like 50 years later. And with any fractal, you can see a hint of the whole shape in all of its parts. And maybe you'll see some of your parts reflected in there too.

And then you'll be screwed because the Patriarch Deity is out to get those crazy people that are turning everything on its head and not buying into his system. If you see him, don't tell Zeus that I'm the one who roasted hot dogs on the branches of the olive tree. But send along our warmest thanks for the kickass place to party.

Professor Cramulus, KSC, ASS

NO RULES ENFORCED
καλλιστι
DISCORDIAN SOCIETY

CHOOSE YOUR OWN ADVENTURE® 5

THE CLASSIC SERIES IS BACK!
CHOOSE FROM 39 POSSIBLE ENDINGS.

The First Day of Fifth Grade

PATRON APOSTLE SRI SYADASTI

The Strange Times

This morning I looked out my window and I saw an unsettling and surreal painting sprawling out to the edge of the sunrise.

Jedi and zombies, vampires and ninjas, cat suits and kings, robots and chameleons, prophets and the profane, and everybody's together, eyes match forward, getting on the train.

We call it the Strange Times.

This is the state of modern living.

We live in a world way weirder than any realm any explorer could ever hope to map. This is a world where your nervous system, tangled with fractals that are creeping like vines, extends its tendrils into the modern jungle.

Rule 34: if it exists, there is pornography involving it. There are lollipops with bugs in them. People get surgery to look exactly like Barbie Dolls. There are humans that have become lizards and tigers. The guys in suits have all become cyborgs. Children don't just play Cowboys and Indians anymore, now they play Self Aware Artificial Intelligence versus the Benevolent Plutocracy.

It's the Strange Times and every human being, even the boring ones, is unspeakably, unknowably weird.

Everybody used to be into the same stuff, you know? Everybody was at cocktail hour, everybody was into the Beatles, everybody was bathing together in the mainstream. But something happened as the stream got quicker, it forked out into a million little tributaries. The mainstream isn't a river anymore, it's an aqueduct and a sewer all at the same time. It's underneath us, always moving, carrying along all these images and symbols and the familiar sound of the ocean. Ideas bump into each other, and sometimes they STICK, and that's how we get things like a music gadget you can masturbate with, or Japanese game shows dubbed with slapstick comedy banter. It's not because these things are good ideas in of themselves, it's because the mainstream keeps juxtaposing these bits of shrapnel in new ways. It's all being churned up, and the whirlpool keeps getting faster.

Nothing has prepared us for the Strange Times.

If you think you can study history and make some educated guess at what's going to happen next, you're dead wrong. Yeah humans are still humans - those poor shit flinging monkeys, trapped inside their nervous systems. When you zoom out, they're not individual drops of water, they're the swell and pulse of a wild ocean. That hasn't changed in six thousand years. But these times are different. There is wholesome sex in bathrooms and righteous violence in the high schools. Kingdoms make war upon each other not by sacking cities, but by cutting deep sea internet cables. Super-memes collide and bounce off each other like sumo wrestlers, every single cell in their bloated bodies contains a lonely and confused human being. Our language is not evolving quick enough to keep pace. Words like "Good", "Evil", "Know", "Learn", and "To Be" are woefully inadequate to describe the modern world. These are the Dangers of Modern Living.

We spent thousands of years living in caves, working the fire and the rock. Then we caught the City virus, and the city spirit used us to build hundreds of temples. We spent generations in the sun, tilling the fields for the Nobles. Then we fled into darkness of the factories, the air choked with the din of industry. In hindsight, it seemed to happen in a predictable way. Thesis, antithesis, synthesis. Build, destroy. Sunrise, sunset. Now we're in the world that doesn't sleep. If it's light here, it's dark somewhere else, like a snake biting its tail. People on the other side of the world are your neighbors, but there is an interminable distance between you and the guy next door (who you've never actually met). You see them every day, but the people on the train will remain strangers, and stranger still.

Odd juxtapositions are the sign of the Strange Times. Comedians are doing impressions of the King. The Catholic Pope looks just like Emperor Palpatine from Star Wars. We sit in the dark around a flickering campfire and listen to the news man tell us stories about the Dangers of Modern Living. The news man knows that when you juxtapose an image with the story, it creates a new meaning which is somewhere in between the ear and the eye. And if we zoom out a tiny bit, the story is juxtaposed with the house that the TV is in. And if we zoom out, that house is inside your head, next to all these other symbols and squiggles and values.

And then at some point, someone thinks it's sexy to dress up like a cartoon cat.

Nobody's prepared us for the Strange Times, and there are literally billions of humans that can't cope with it. They could deal with being serfs, they could deal with being soldiers, those are simple lives with simple choices. Now it's come time to make a new story for themselves by assembling all these weird symbols into a lifestyle, a personality, a set of values. And they just don't know how to do it. They look to culture to get clues for how to swim and be happy and break even in this weird world, and all they see are porn models and ninja turtles and humane terrorism and the extreme left and the extreme right and nothing is centered.

If it was as simple as dealing with the sun and the crops, however hard that might be, people would pull through and maintain. But there are a million choices and complexities and nuances and shrapnel flying at you like throwing knives and pillow fights and semen and banana cream pies.

We think it's best to laugh.

WHAT MOVIE AM I IN?
WHAT TRIP IS THE THEATER ON?
WHAT CAN I DO ABOUT IT?

A. Chaos

The most extensive program of alleged "domestic spying" by CIA on Americans was the "CHAOS" program. CHAOS was the centerpiece of a major CIA effort begun in 1967 in response to White House pressure for intelligence about foreign influence upon American dissent. The CHAOS mission was to gather and evaluate all available information about foreign links to racial, antiwar and other protest activity in the United States. CHAOS was terminated in 1974.

The CHAOS office participated in the preparation of some half dozen major reports for higher authorities, all of which concluded that no significant role was being played by foreign elements in the various protest movements. This repeatedly negative finding met with continued skepticism from the White House under two administrations and pressures for further inquiry. In response to this skepticism CHAOS continued to expand its coverage of Americans in order to increase White House confidence in the accuracy of its findings.

A second major element of the CHAOS operation was to pursue specific inquiries from the FBI about the activity of particular Americans traveling abroad.

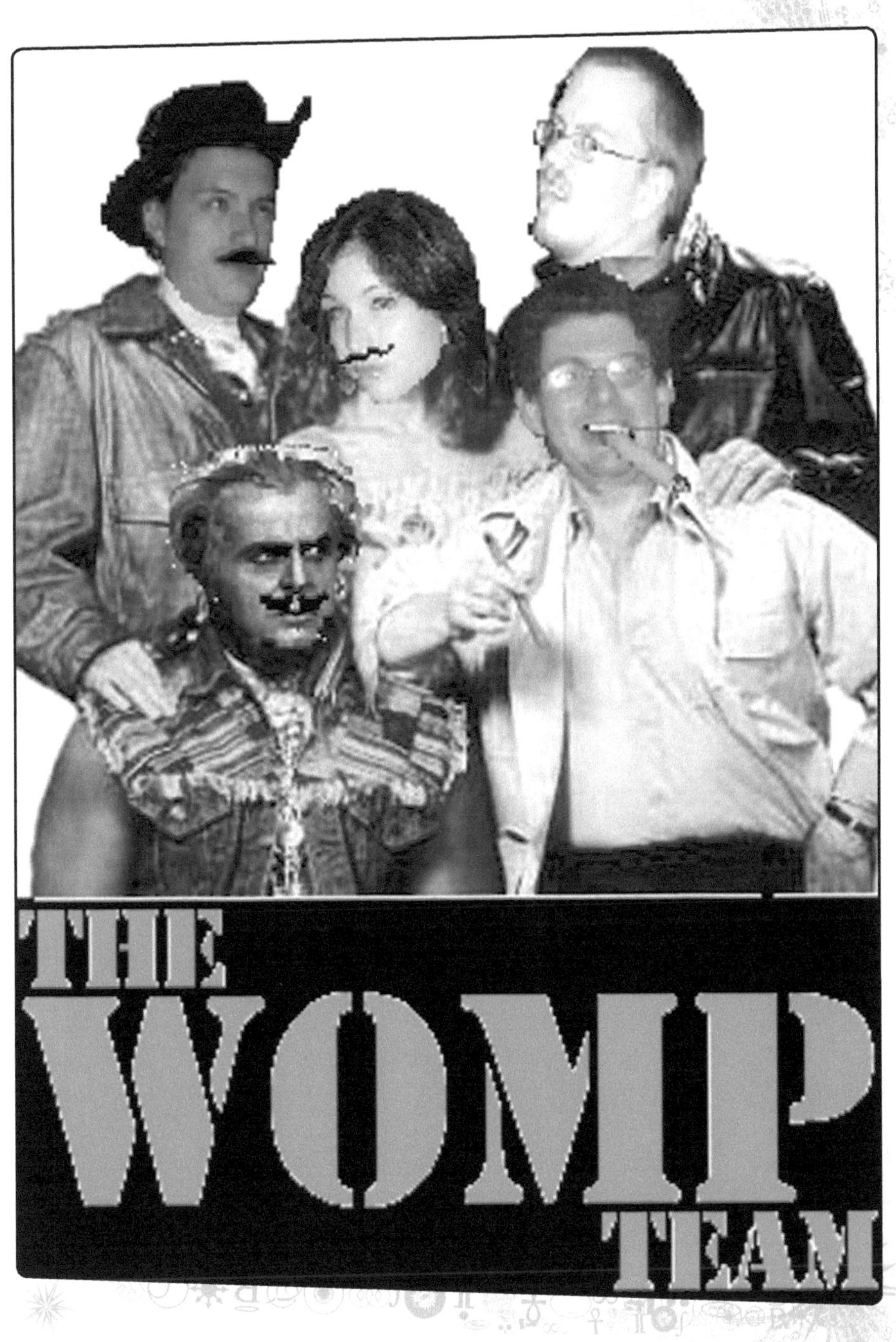
THE
WOMP
TEAM

THE ILLUSIONS ARE TRYING TO CHANGE YOU.
CHANGE YOURSELF AS YOU PLEASE. DETERMINATION AND PERSISTENCE IS GREAT QUALITY IN THE LONG RUN. YOU CAN CHANGE THE ILLUSIONS. USE YOUR IMAGINATION AND WILL POWER TO CHANGE. EVOLVE YOUR DREAM.

TAZ Has Ugly Retarded Cousin

The Temporary Totalitarian Zone is the Machine's answer to the Temporary Autonomous Zone. The idea is that within a matter of hours, an entire city can go from normal Monday afternoon to crawling with heavily armed paramilitary police, and hours after that, they disappear into the ether as quickly as they swarmed in. Designed to reinforce the false notion that the Police really can be everywhere at once, the TTZ is a system of roving police states capable of springing up anywhere at almost a moment's notice in order to assist the powers that be in whatever devious plot they have at a given moment.

In a "post-9/11 world", as we are all constantly reminded we are living in, the vast majority of rubes living out there in la-la land actually welcome the TTZ as it storms down Main Street, feeling extra safe from Terrorists, but never quite catching on to the fact that all it takes is one terse command from the lips of some fat asshole in Washington, and all those guns can be aiming directly at the heads of "innocent" civilians.

Of course, at that point, We the People would probably turn ourselves in for being Terrorists without even knowing we were up to no good.

Anyway, being that the TTZ is a tool for totalitarian schmucks, it is not going to stop here. No, expect the TTZs to increase in duration and frequency until it reaches a point where the Police really are everywhere at once.

Bare Minimum →

Like *You*...
THE BEARER OF THIS CARD
IS A **PRISONER** OF HIS or HER
OWN **PRIVATE**

Black Iron Prison

AND WE ARE INVITING
YOU TO A **JAIL BREAK.**

Every man, woman and child on this Earth is an inmate of their own **Black Iron Prison**.
You cannot escape, but your life experience, your 'cell,' can be altered drastically.
~ This is known, ironically, as **'The Jail Break.'** ~
Reproduce and distribute these cards freely | BIP Headquarters: **blackironprison.com**

Bare Minimum BIP as recovered from an ancient manuscript in the archives of Semi Secret Order Of Kabbalistic Navigators (SSOOKN).

1. What you think of as REALITY is a collection of ideas and beliefs about REALITY. Many of the ideas you have about REALITY come from the culture in which you were raised and have accumulated haphazardly over time.
2. This, in itself, is not a problem. The problem is in forgetting point number 1. When you forget point 1, you mistake your ideas about reality for being REALITY itself. Of this, it has been said 'the menu is not the meal'. Please refrain from eating the menu.
3. People who 'eat the menu' frequently become confused and annoyed when other people insist on seeing REALITY in a different way. All that truly differs are their ideas and beliefs about REALITY.
4. Beliefs are just thoughts you keep having.
5. No living being is capable of perceiving all of REALITY, as all senses of perception are limited. Humans can only see, hear, smell, taste and feel within certain parameters. Information entering our senses undergoes compression, filtration, and distortion, before interpretation. Interpretation is what happens when information meets your 'beliefs'.
6. For no good reason, we call this composite of Belief & Biological Limits THE BLACK IRON PRISON and is a metaphor about existence. It means that there is very little you can do about biology; however, you can choose what becomes part of your beliefs. (Always keeping point 1 in mind).

7. Each person exists within their own, unique BIP 'cell'. The cell is composed of the following:
   a) Biological limits – these are largely unchangeable. b) Belief systems – these are highly changeable. Because of (a) the BIP cell cannot be escaped. Because of (b) your life experience, your 'cell', can be altered drastically. This is what we try to call 'reconstruction'.
8. A life long commitment to continual reconstruction is known, ironically, as 'The Jail Break'. Reconstruction is HARD WORK.
9. The collection of beliefs, thoughts, notions etc that form your cell are all equally VALID, though none are TRUE in the sense that they "are" REALITY. However, some beliefs and ideas are more useful than others in specific situations. It is up to the individual to decide which beliefs and ideas they should employ in a given situation.
10. Some people believe that the term BLACK IRON PRISON is dark, bleak, depressing and even frightening. If you prefer, use the term GOLDEN SPHERE of POSSIBILITY (GSP) instead. It means exactly the same thing as BIP and all points still apply.
11. BIP (or GSP) can be philosophical antidote to dogmatism.

You are cordially invited to a Jail Break.

You know you're being watched. Fuck off with your "this is more conspiracy theory garbage" reactions.

This is the truth.

They have cameras, man. The smoke detector in your hotel room is wired. They make cell phone manufacturers put GPS units in every single model, even if they don't use it as a selling point. Just imagine what's in your car. They're onto you, don't doubt that. But so what? If they're going to follow you around and take notes, the least you can do is make sure their investment is worthwhile.

The following will help you to increase the value your tax dollars get:

1. Make conflicting reservations at different hotels at opposite ends of the country, and on that night, sleep in the park under a surveillance camera. Also, if you're too loaded with cash and have nothing better to do, book a one-way ticket to Morocco and never get on the plane.
2. Commit a misdemeanor. These assholes want files on everybody, and if they don't have anything they will make one up. If you get booked for littering or shoplifting a pack of gum, then you're a petty criminal. If they have nothing on you at all, you might end up being a Terrorist Mastermind.
3. Prank-call 911 from pay phones in the rich neighborhoods.
4. Buy things on the Internet from people in Third-World countries. It doesn't matter what it is, as long as it isn't a rug.
5. When going through security checkpoints, embellish your cell phone with nonfunctional wires and switches.
6. With a couple of friends in separate vehicles, organize a pursuit of a DHS van through downtown.
7. Buy a copy of Catcher in the Rye, but sell it on eBay.
8. When you sign for purchases on electronic card-reading devices, sign the words HELLO NSA.

These steps will accomplish nothing, but they will make you feel like a secret operative, fighting a war you don't understand for people who don't even know you exist. And in lieu of any real freedoms, the illusion of participation in your own demise should be considered a civil right.

A BANTAM BOOK * 13978-9 * $1.50 *

CHOOSE YOUR OWN ADVENTURE™ • 7

YOU'RE THE STAR OF THE STORY!
CHOOSE FROM 38 POSSIBLE ENDINGS.

Discordians Take Over Outer Space

BY PATRON APOSTLE HUNG MUNG

ILLUSTRATED BY YUO

00021

GAY WANGO
TANGO ROOM

DO NOT DISTURB
THE DANCERS

THE WORLD'S GREATEST METAPHOR:
A giant inflatable dog turd created by the American artist Paul McCarthy was blown from its moorings at a Swiss museum, bringing down a power line and breaking a window before landing in the grounds of a children's home. Go on, see how many world events or people you can apply it to. Its amazing.

Dream Jams in the Bird Theater

BY 5HROOM BOB PENTA PANTZ AND ZARATHUD

A little discordian game: Picture all events, scenes, moments in life stuffed on top of one another like the bricks in strange giant Tetris -- all existing Now. If you need to create a traffic jam, car chaos, or an escape route for some reason, but you don't want to risk your neck, and have no money to spend - WE HAVE A SOLUTION.

Picture your self as an eye moving upwards (all roads lead to the top...) on your own subjective experience trip, in your own continuum. Make sure the square has some birds hanging around. Pidgeons and seagulls are great. Make sure you're familliar with the area, in case you need to get out quickly.

Answer: Who is the Camera? Who is the Actor? Who is the Director? Who is the Writer? Who comes up with the plays? Who chose the scenery? Start out by feeding the birds with bread. Gather a larger number of birds. If you do this for a few days in a row, more birds are sure to show up for a free meal. Answer: What movie am I in? What trip is the theater on?

What can I do about it?

Throw the bread closer and closer to the action zone.

To initiate the attack, change yourself as you please. Determination and persistence is great quality in the long run. You can change the illusions. Use your Imagination and Will Power to change/evolve your dream. And after getting the first car to stop, the cars behind it stop too!

Attraction and distraction keeps things in your dream (love & hate etc). By Accepting things. they pass on. Not accepting tend to make them come back. Bombard the road and cars with more bread, grain, and other bird food. You are your own imagination. You chose who you are all the time, in every event. Change as you please - but those not living in the Now will probably counterfeit quick changes. Their scree's and callings will make more and more birds to come, adding to the chaos.

"WHO THE FUCK IS KEEPING THE LOVE HOSTAGE, MAN?!"

—DR. STRANGELOVE OR HOW I LEARNED TO STOP WORRYING AND LOVE THE ATOM BOMB

BY PRINCESS MADNONYMUS

The Expanse of the Universe and other such Preposterous Perceptions
God created Adam unto the Earth
And with a French kiss, tongues touching, he gave him the breath of life

Adam shrugged and stretched and let out a yawn
He scratched his bum and let out a fart
He said: You will do this in memory of me

The Universe, a whole organic entity endowed with an exquisite sense of aesthetics and a mightily attuned sense of smell, took offence of such behavior
And, away from this pungent prickly unshaven individual, so rude, so started the expanse of the Universe.

The redshift when examining far away star
Is a result of the universe holding its breath for the smell

This shall be known as the Original Fart (by those in the know)
Or the Big Bang (for those left guessing)

In his defense, Adam had one thing to say
Shit makes the flowers grow and that is beautiful
Chill out man!, he thought, We have a long ways to go...

In the garden of Eden, God gave many advice to Adam
One being "Be careful what you wish for, you WILL get it."
And so Eve came to be ...

Upon entering Eden, Eve misheard "Expanse of the Universe" for "Expensive Universe", so instead of heading straight home, she hurried to the shopping mall and bought these serpent leather shoes she saw on sale at Cromagnon's stand.

Left to himself without any meal prepared for supper, Adam wonderd and pondered
Man, do I feel hungover! This whole being created thing is rougher than it appears!
What was it that weird voice in my head said about this red fruit here ...
Let's see ...

How bizarre! Only half a worm seems to live in this apple!
Where could the other half be?
That does not feel like a Contended Chao

This was the first Erisian mysteree that man confronted

It was to be solved quickly when Eve came back home
Idiot! said Eve You ate the other half of the worm!
Can't you be more careful?
You should wash your fruits and vegetables before eating them.
You are forbidden from eating off of this three ever again.

Heavy!, thought Adam, I will be in the field crushing rotten berries ...
If I am to be stuck in this paradise place for long, I need to figure out that alcohol thing quick.

And so the search rages on....

When will we leave the Garden?

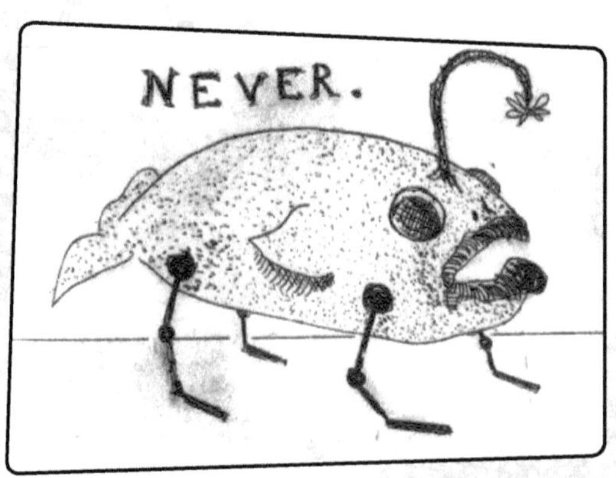

How it Will Happen

BY ENRICO SALAZAR

While Enrico was bent over last night, clipping toenails, it came. The fantastic vision he had been waiting his entire life for. The way to take over. Get back what was Enrico's. What will be Enrico's again.

Let Enrico paint a visual picture for all you beautiful faggots.

It begins with the national bird of Salazore; the Ostrich. We don't actually have any Ostriches on Salazore, but then again we don't have any birds at all, other than turkey vultures, and they don't make a very nice image on a postage stamp, so the ostrich was adopted. It begins with Ostriches.

The second ingredient is over-the-top transvestites. Or drag queens, if you prefer that term. On Salazore they were called Brujadellos, and every boy lost his bip-bip to one. Enrico lost his to five of them. What a night. Anyway. The second ingredient is Brujadellos, and lots of them.

The third ingredient is pump-action shotguns. One for each transvestite. Enrico will, of course, be holding his own beauty of a weapon, a Sturmgewehr 44 named Skippy he has had since he grew moss on his rolling stones.

Imagine. Imagine thousands of transvestites, mounted on Ostrich-back, storming into each major city. Imagine. Imagine the frozen citizens, staring at the twisted beauty of these animals. Imagine. Imagine, if you will, the carnage when each gun is opened up. Imagine the confusion. Imagine the disorder. Imagine the possibilities.

As the madness reaches a frenzy Enrico strides in on his Ostrich, decked in full Salazorian military regalia; dripping from gherri-curl to curly-haired toes in flags, pins, buttons, and diamonds. Mirror sunglasses, vaseline on mustachio, sneer on lips. Arms raised into the air. Cheers, jeers, queers. Everything Enrico loves.

It's enough to make a faggot break down in giggling sniffly sobs.

It will be goddam beautiful, my fuckers. It will be fantastic, my mofos. And, you will all be welcome in Salazore when the fighting is over, Enrico is back on his fold-up chair and people are done kicking and gouging in the mud, the blood, and the beer.

Если что-нибыдь, то я могу сделать для того чтобы убедить вас, скажите мне путь. Я взобрался бы самая высокая гора, плаваю самый глубокий океан, ползание через самое глубокое и самое темное подземелье как раз к горбу аа из вас.

BY REVEREND WHAT'S-HIS-NAME?

The Black Iron Prison is a collection of essays by various authors discussing such topics as free will, self-liberation, and coping with the madness of the modern era. In this piece, Rev. What's-His-Name discusses the origins of the Black Iron Prison.

It was the year 2006. I imagine it was another initiate to the principiadiscordia.com realm that started it all by saying something like, "Well, if you guys are so interested in moving beyond the Principia Discordia, why don't you guys write something?!" Well, maybe it wasn't exactly like that, but it sounds nice so I'll go with it. What's important is that a bunch of us got to the point where we decided it was time for us to take a stab at this Discordia thing. And so, the project was dubbed "PD06". There was a feeling amongst many at PD that while the subject matter of the Principia was still important, the jokes were, by now, were old, and not as useful as they used to be. We were interested in boiling down some of the ideas and putting them in a form where newer generations of Discordians could grasp onto them. (It's generally not advised to grab ANYTHING that is boiling. Turn your handles in.) We decided to circle around this idea of the Black Iron Prison that we had been discussing. LMNO wrote an intro piece about the BIP which really set the tone for what would follow.

And so we were off. Some people wrote new things, some found old things and added new bits to it. The inspiration was quite catchy and in a matter of days we had a pamphlet's worth of material. The next step was to put it together into a sexy and attractive package. The ever-crafty LMNO sacrificed his lunch hour to put it together and thus The Black Iron Prison: Discordia Revisited was born. Rev. St. Syn, KSC added an attention-grabbing graphic to the cover and it was released to the masses. Since its completion, we've continued to discuss various philosophies and ideas within the Black Iron Prison framework. Indeed, yours truly started up a forum dedicated to the Black Iron Prison subject matter. But it went kerplooey and so it now resides as a part of PrincipiaDiscordia.com. Professor Cramulus has since re-edited the pamphlet into a second version. Both versions, along with the other Black Iron Prison project materials, can be found at:

http://www.blackironprison.com

—and—

http://www.principiadiscordia.com/bip/1.php

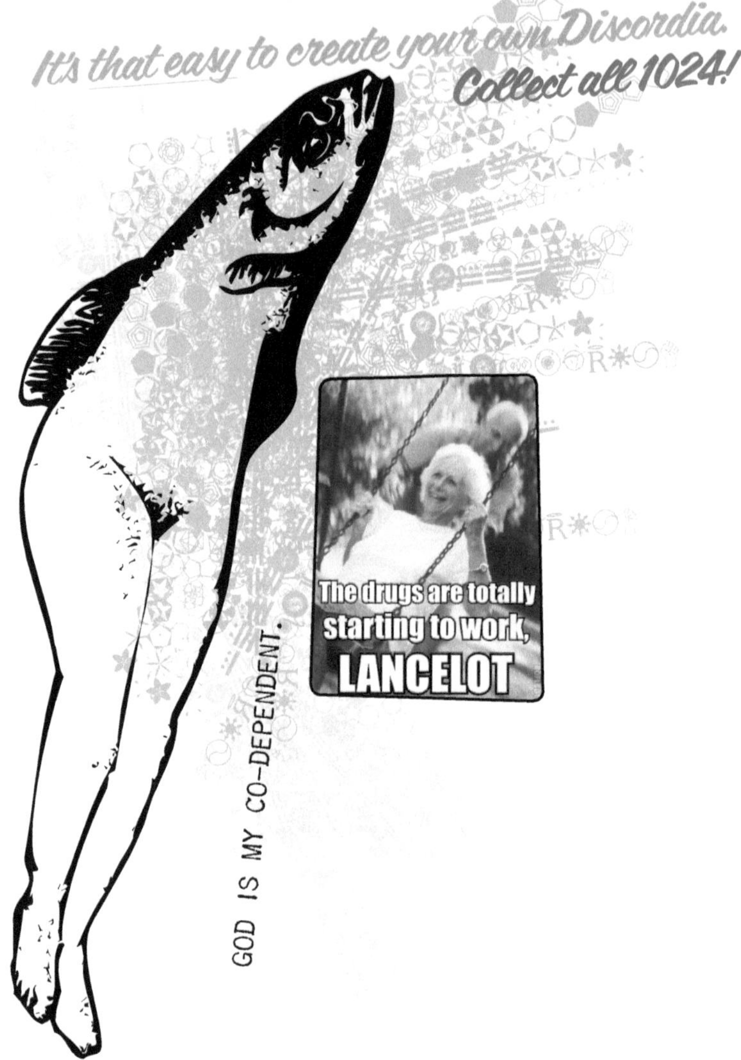

5 Minutes of Panic

BY UNDUE, DIRTYESSENCE, AND EDITING BY ZARATHUD

"So do you got any ideas about the report next week?"

The trance was broken, with poor word selection no less. As those thoughts echoed in the mind, my mouth, still performing basic social functions for some odd reason, responded in a negative colloquialism. Tony was a cool guy I guess, good in the common sense of the word, the kind of kid you'd be proud to have as your son. We're Discordians, not the army.

"So you've crawled out of the darkness into our fold?"

He tried to sell it with a chuckle, I wasn't in the mood to purchase pleasantries.

"You don't have to prove yourself to us. You don't need to latch onto our buzzwords and repeat our memes to show that you're in. You don't need to proselytize. You don't need to rebel against your former life, purge it with fire and devote every moment to throwing yourself against the System."

The drudgery, the sheer intolerable drudgery.

He glanced at my file. "Oh so you live where?"

Who gives a shit where I live honestly? My name is the least important thing about me or anybody for that matter. Fuck this.

"All we really ask you to do is laugh a little more. Think a little more. Explore a little more in places you usually wouldn't go. Talk to strangers. Listen to strangers. Do a few of those things that you thought might be neat but filed away with a 'maybe someday'. And whatever you do, don't get complacent.

"Bob", will this bus never stop? Trail it off, make your response times slower and slower, the thing will die naturally. "Oh, and keep your eyes peeled for the Goddess." Another chuckle. Why do people think that will improve a substance free and impersonal comment?

As I got off the bus, his words chilled me,

"You'll know Her when you see Her."

"Yeah," I shouted to the people on the bus, "Chances are, She will be laughing at you."

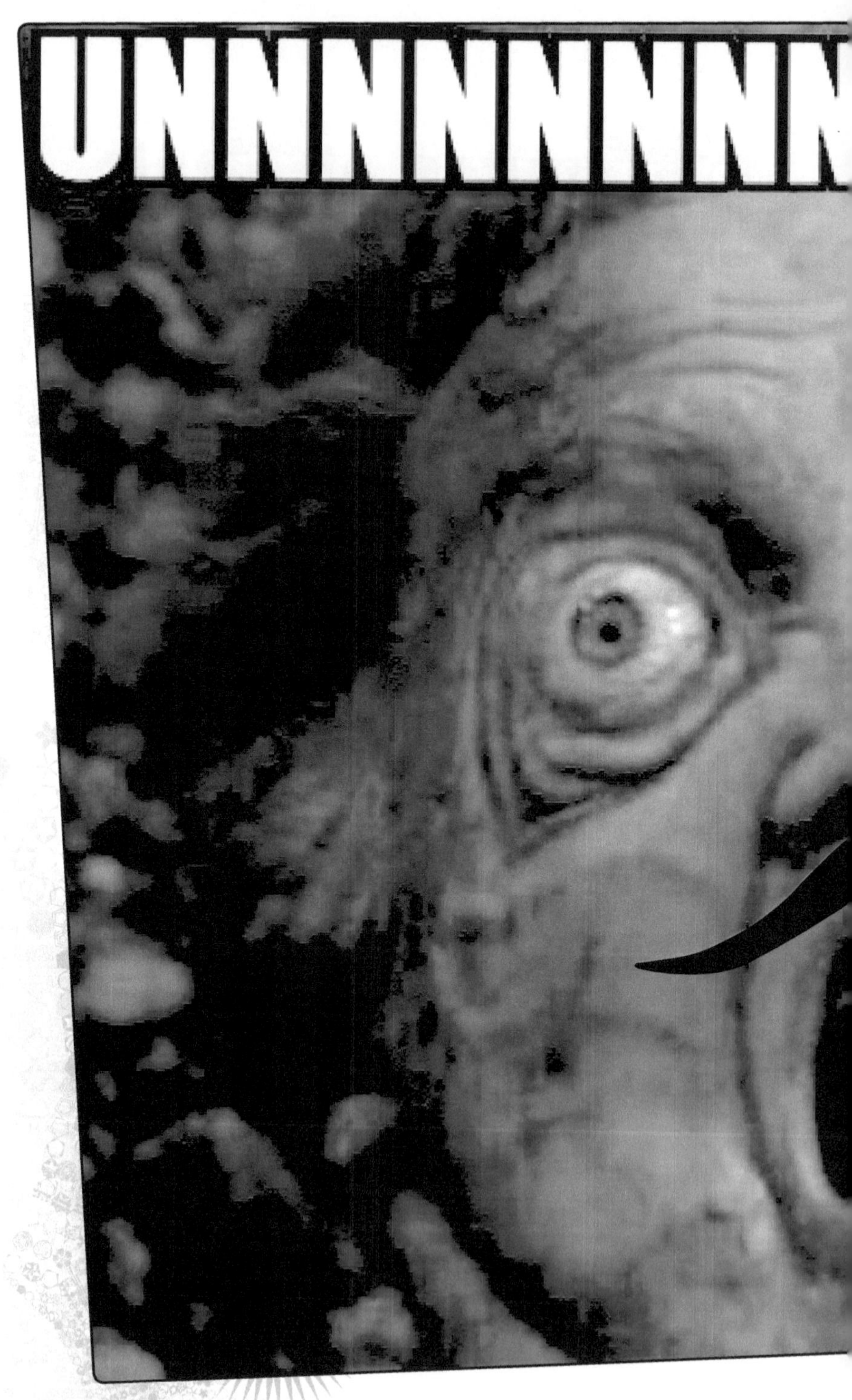
UNNNNNNNNN

NNNNNNNNNG!

You are your own imagination.

You chose who you are all the time, every event occurring. Change as you please - but those not living in the Now will probably counterfeit quick changes. Continue to choose the same for stability.

Go Mindfuck Yourself
or
Be the Trouble You Want to See in the World

> Celine reared back as if I had waved offal under his nose. "Objectivists?" he pronounced the word as if I had accused him of being a child-molester. "We're anarchists and outlaws, goddam it. Didn't you understand that much? We've got nothing to do with right-wing, left-wing or any other half-assed political category. If you work within the system, you come to one of the either/or choices that were implicit in the system from the beginning. You're talking like a medieval serf, asking the first agnostic whether he worships God or the Devil. We're outside the system's categories. You'll never get the hang of our game if you keep thinking in flat-earth imagery of right and left, good and evil, up and down. If you need a group label for us, we're political non-Euclideans. But even that's not true. Sink me, nobody of this tub agrees with anybody else about anything, except maybe what the fellow with the horns told the old man in the clouds: Non serviam." —Robert Anton Wilson, Illuminatus!

Eris loves activists.

Here in the Strange Times, there's a million billion crawly little critters trying to ride you down the river. See, you're floating through chaotic, shrapnel filled rapids. The foamy waters are brimming with symbols and images and squiggles and good causes. It's easy to cling to one like a life preserver and ride it for all its worth. You're clinging to some right now. You are a sticky meme, and you're trying to stay afloat. It's only human.

The first part of the Golden Secret is to Let Go.

You grabbed onto that symbol and that in-joke and that good cause because they were at the right place at the right time. When you're receptive, it's convenient to get on a raft made of religion or politics or some other made-up ideology. It's easy to assemble an identity out of tastes and values and shrapnel floating by. Over time, some of that stuff stops supporting your weight. Right when you're about to go under, you reach out and grab onto some other piece of shrapnel. You cling to it and use it to hold your head above the waters. At some point, you saw some stuff and met some people, and their shtick appealed to you, and you internalized it, and now you think that stuff is a part of you.

Fast forward to the present: you're riding down the river in a barrel, your knuckles white as they grip your life preservers. Your pockets are stuffed with photographs, and there's cultural water in your ears. Let GO already. You don't need that crap. That's somebody else's crap. Learn to swim on your own.

The second part of the Golden Secret is to Ignite Yourself, While There's Still Time.

I'm advocating activities. Not activism, but activitism. I don't recommend you go find a cause (or some other baggage) to serve, I'm recommending you get up, get out, and DO something. They've got you whipped like a circus lion to watch the world and then react to it. They want you to be a passive observer. The face on the money has you trained like Pavlov's dog. That's how the Machine works. It's made of perfectly predictable parts.

You could get bored. You could get numb. You could be alone in a sea of people. These are the Dangers of Modern Living.

There's something out there which will make you excited just to wake up in the morning, and it's not spending your hard earned money on the latest You've-Gotta-See-This blockbuster. That shrapnel is just a distraction. The voices of the cultural chorus are a distraction too, because really, you're not one of Them.

You're a freak. You're weird in ways not even your best friends can understand. This is the Strange Times, and there are no groups of people, only individuals standing next to each other.

There's somebody in your life who you look to for direction. The one with the plan. The one who has great ideas. The one who seems to know what's going on. Kill him. Take his job. Become him. Quit waiting for somebody else to come up with something fun to do. Quit waiting for rock bottom or some other excuse

to change what you don't like about yourself. Cough up all the water in your lungs and BREATHE you'll drown if you don't BREATHE for the first time ever BREATHE.

This isn't a lesson you can learn once and internalize. This is an ongoing challenge to *constantly reinvent yourself*. This is a never ending battle you must wage against your comfort and your identity. If you think you've learned this lesson, then you stink of complacency. Initiation never ends.

Keep moving. Stay kinetic. Be the trouble you want to see in the world.

Go Operation Mindfuck yourself.

Hail Eris

Hey Asshole

Humans are assholes. We want to dominate each other, we get off on power-tripping, we're all pissed off that slavery is "wrong." Every last one of us is constantly calculating everybody else's demise, and none of us are immune. The "nice guys" are up to something, the "peacemakers" are just fighting a different kind of war, the prophets talk nice, until somebody offs them, and then heads roll. Even your sweet old granny was playing you. How do you think she lived so long? She was draining the life force out of all the relatives you never met for 50 years. You always knew there was something in her chocolate chip cookies and now you know what it was.

We have seven billion complete assholes piled on top of each other, all of them talking bullshit and committing indiscriminate acts of psychotic manipulation. You think that can lead to anywhere good? Of course not. It leads to a whole planet covered in disease, war, poverty, and all the other shit those do-gooders interrupt late-night TV to complain about. And you hit the mute button when that shit comes on, don't you. See? You're an asshole, just like me.

And not only are people assholes, they're also stupid. In fact, we are tied for intelligence with dolphins.

Fucking DOLPHINS.

And, after a hundred thousand years of people being shitty to each other, we have reached the point now where we can, with the click of a button, wipe everyone and everything off the face of this ball of dirt we call home. You think that at some point, some dickwad isn't going to actually DO IT? Face it. Humanity is the crowning achievement of evolution — and if you've been paying attention you'll see that evolution is an asshole, too.

What do you think is gonna happen? What is the cumulative effect of seven billion angry, distrustful, petty, stingy, half-retarded hairless apes who have nothing better to do than kill each other over stupid things like sneakers and imaginary friends? You think that one day, they're all going to see the light and join hands and say I'm sorry? If that's what you beleive, then you need to get some tinfoil and duct tape and build an impenetrable fortress out of sofa cushions in your living room because you are just the sort of person that natural selection is aiming for.

In the end, it's all going to come down to the very thing you're already imagining and have been imagining since the first time you looked at the Evening News. And you know it, so quit deluding yourself into thinking there's something better worth defending.

It's a sideshow out there, and you're the freak. So quit buzzing around the office all fucking day chit-chatting with people you can't really stand, and find your reason to care whether there's a tomorrow or not. Because the way I see it, really caring about something other than your car or your bank account is the only shot this fucked up species has at survival.

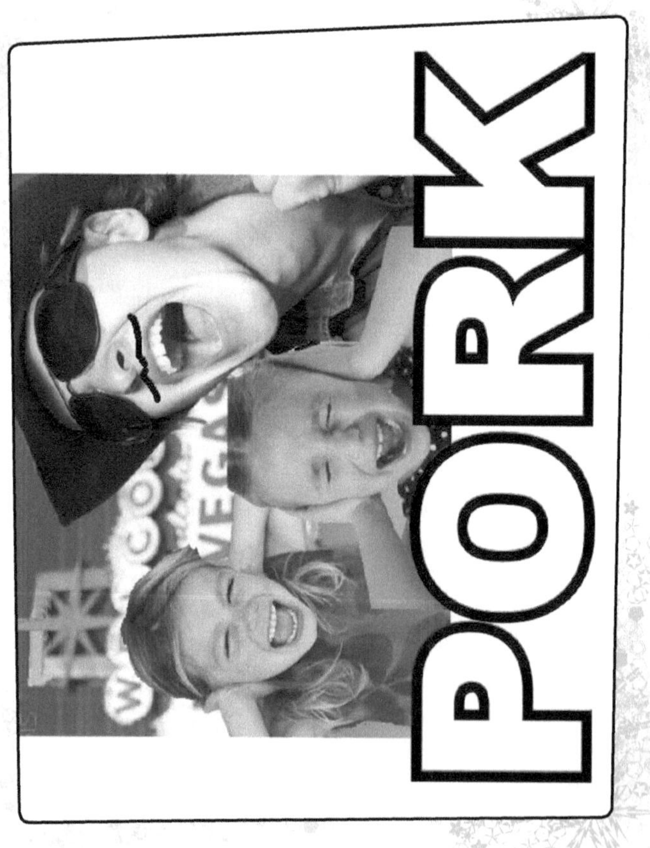

I'm so goth people refer to my heart as an angel graveyard.

I'm so goth I give suicide lessons.

I'm so goth I'm not even goth anymore

I'm so goth my tears destroyed the Roman empire.

Yo mama's so goth you were still born.

I'm so goth I'm dead

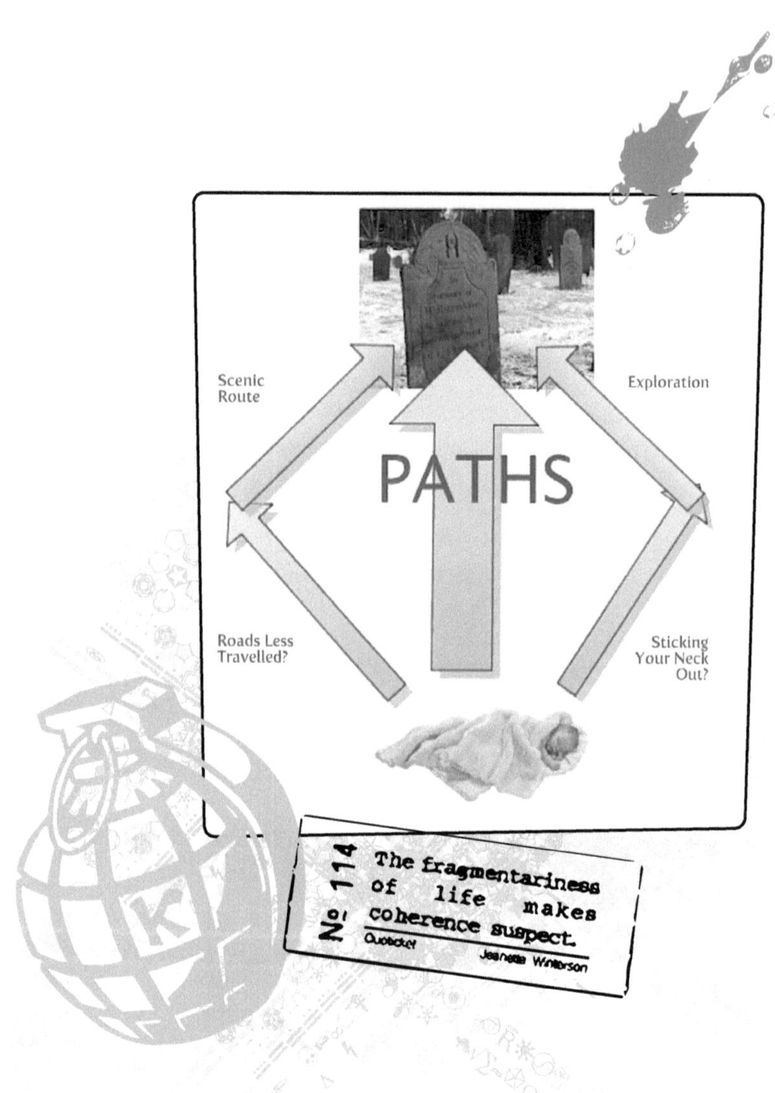
Scenic
Route
Exploration
PATHS
Roads Less
Travelled?
Sticking
Your Neck
Out?
No 114
The fragmentariness
of life makes
coherence suspect.
Quotacket
Jeanette Winterson

BY REV. WHAT'S-HIS-NAME?

Something that can be found at the BIP wiki. It's an exploration of the pathways we take in life and what influences the choices we make. It's an exploration through visuals and written form. Enjoy and post your own thoughts, musings, questions, etc.

Birth and Death are 100% Grade A Certainties (oh yeah taxes too, or so the saying goes). The only questions seem to be around matters of when and how. We know we emerge from our Mother, in some fashion, and then return to the Earth at some undetermined place and time. But we know it WILL happen.

We burst into the world at Point A, birth. Or sometimes we have to be pulled out depending on our level of infantile stubbornness. Immediately we set foot at the beginning of a Path. It is one of many Paths that eventually lead to Point B. At Point B we may exit in a brilliant flash of flame and sound. One of our vital life-sustaining mechanisms may crap out. Or perhaps someone will bring a bloody war to our land and we die in a house to house cleansing. Of course, it also might be something as unceremonious as having a heart-attack in the middle of a massive bowel movement. But hey, shit happens right?

In any event, we have before us a series of roads to take to get to Point B. Of course, as young infants we really don't have a clear concept of Point B, so it initially doesn't really inform our Path. Well, there are natural fight or flight responses like "Feed Me." But it's really focused more around infantile narcissm than it is any actual fear of starving to death. Indeed, as kiddos we see that damn Coyote fall off the cliff a zillion times and he keeps on breathing. So the worst that might happen to us is we turn into an accordion for a few seconds. As we grow, however, we establish more control and more responsibility for our own orienteering. At every step of the way (or maybe it's every other step, I'm not entirely sure. It would be quite a feat if anyone figured it out), it seems, there is a new turn that can be taken; left, right, left-right. Which do we choose? Why do we choose? Are we even aware of it?

Along the paths there is another phenomenon that is occuring. As we are walking our Paths, and deciding where to go (whether through instince, deliberate thought process, because someone told us so), we are subjected to, and subjecting others to, Shrapnel.

Shrapnel are the bits of experience, events, ideas, and so on that are flying around as we walk the Paths. It's as though there are roadside bombs that are in a continuous state of detonation. For example, we walk along the path as a young child, and at a certain point, we are subjected to Religious Shrapnel. Whether or not to follow our parents' deities? Whether or not to NOT follow deities? Whether or not to follow a deity different from our family's? Whether or not I'll burn in hell if I don't eat the cracker? As we are approaching the age of 18, we experience Shrapnel from education and career. Guidance counselors are asking you if you want to attend the college fairs. Your Dad is asking you if you are going to that ivy-league college he did. Or perhaps your Mom runs a flower shop and is expecting you to take over. After all, it is called Me and My Daughter's Blooms. But do you really want to peddle flowers the rest of your life?

There are, of course many, many other examples of Shrapnel. Also. it is important to understand that we aren't passive bystanders in all of this. We too are part of the Shrapnel creating process. When we become parents we subject our children to expectations, wishes, and wants for their lives. (If all parents' wishes for their children actually came true, we'd be living in a world comprised solely of Doctors and Lawyers. You'd never be able to get onto a golf course.) As neighbors, we may be part of a collective attitude about how people's houses and yards should look. (Oh look, Sanderson is putting out another fucking Pink Flamingo. And gosh, it looks like it is fellating the Garden Gnome! Gasp!) As members of Political Party X, we put signs in our yard saying, vote for Rudy Obama. We are throwing out just as much as others are throwing at us.

Do not be disillusioned about Shrapnel. It isn't all bad. There is the Shrapnel of Art and Creativity. Walking by a park and seeing some folks drumming and creating music. (Drum Circles aren't just for hippies anymore.) The infective beat that is travelling across the air, that mandates that you move and groove. The lady down the road who is a brilliant artist, displaying her work at the local Sidewalk Art Exhibit. There is the Shrapnel of Happy Childlike Anarchy. Your little girl acting like a goon, and you can't help but to want to play along. Experiencing the joy in improvisational imagination and going with the flow. This is the sort of Shrapnel you WANT embedded in your flesh. For it too will inform your path. And besides, when you ARE strolling on your path, wouldn't it be more enjoyable if you were doing a little jig along the way, while whistling a fun little tune? Whistle while you walk. It seemed to do the trick for the Dwarvish 7.

So what to take away from this? Well, first off, make sure you read the other observations of Shrapnel. And then, take a few minutes and think about your path. Think about where you've been, who've you encountered, what you put in your mouth (ewww, you did that?), and how've you navigated life thus far. As you think of the different experiences you've had, think of what might have happened if you hadn't had those experiences. Caution: the point isn't to think about how you could re-write your life. That part's done, no good to dwell on it. But, how can you use this perspective going forward? What kind of mental armor can you obtain to shield you from that which may blow you off course? What kind of mechanisms can you construct to welcome in those things in this world which may benefit you? Or better yet, how can you have more bearing on your bearings?

Because seriously, you know Point B is coming soon. Why not make it one hell of a ride?

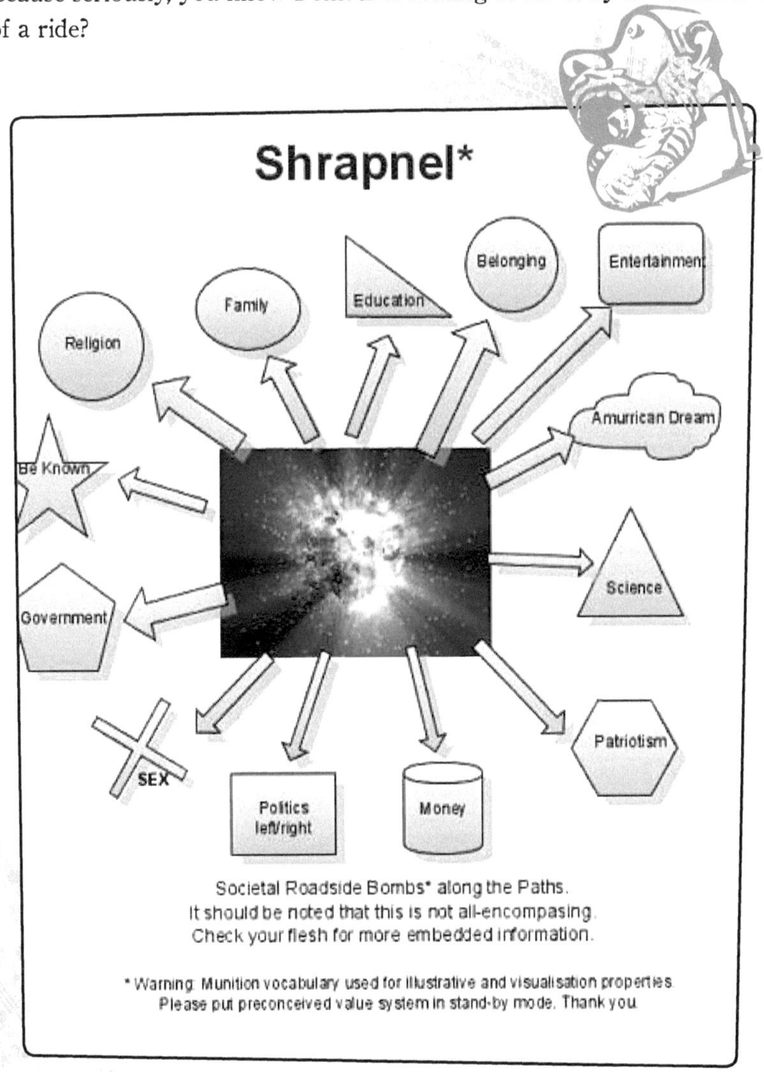

Shrapnel*

Religion
Family
Education
Belonging
Entertainment
Amurrican Dream
Be Known
Science
Government
Patriotism
SEX
Politics left/right
Money

Societal Roadside Bombs* along the Paths.
It should be noted that this is not all-encompasing.
Check your flesh for more embedded information.

* Warning: Munition vocabulary used for illustrative and visualisation properties.
Please put preconceived value system in stand-by mode. Thank you.

FAITH CAN MOVE MOUNTAINS AND FLY PLANES INTO BUILDINGS.

THOU ART WHOLE

BY LHX

i will propose the notion here that the shrapnel being discussed lately has an identifiable source

it is the result of people under pressure

i will propose also that pressure is the result of confronting fear or desire

fear is generally associated with death (the unknown - the potential for physical pain) or an injury to the ego that would have social repercussions (which could also be potentially indirectly related to death)

desire is generally associated with avoiding that which causes fear, but also social achievement (striving to rule the kingdom of physical objects)

also stimulation

these elements set people in motion

when coming face-to-face with a fear or with the possibility of not obtaining a desire - we find explosions people cannot handle the pressure and there is a resulting action

in its raw form - this action is generally not premeditated

- you scare the shit out of somebody - and it is understandable that the gut instinct is to yell

but now,

we live in a situation where people can be elaborate when they explode

people "take it out on" other people

being overwhelmed in one facet of life - you take it out in another facet of life

a fear of death results in a fundamentalist tunnel-vision

getting cock-blocked in early adolescence spawns a generation of computer programmers looking for social comeuppance, while subsequently pushing humanity to its technological demise

the slums of New York results in the greatest Hip Hop in 25,000 years

and this here what you're reading - this is my shrapnel

this is my outlet

i've read a lot of RAW shit and some other alternative approaches to psychology. but a few months ago, in my first semester of college, something struck me when i was forced to take an 'intro to psychology' course

one segment of the course dealt with 'defense mechanisms'

apparently - there is a term which describes what is known as basically the one productive defense mechanism

it is called sublimation

i just looked it up at m-w.com: "to divert the expression of (an instinctual desire or impulse) from its unacceptable form to one that is considered more socially or culturally acceptable"

when we took a look at sublimation in class - there was another aspect to it -

the expression of the 'impulse' was not necessarily 'acceptable' - but it was productive

it was not a defense mechanism that focused on covering things up or hiding things

it was the defense mechanism that sought to transform

turn that negative stimulus causing you pressure into something that can reap benefits

the whole 'lemon -----> lemonade' approach to things

its a bit too trite of a metaphor to use when discussing some of the foul shit life doles out on the mammals running around the surface of this place

its hard to say that hurricane katrina was like 'life handing you lemons' but to stick with that metaphor for a second - these days when life hands people lemons - most of the time people just pick them up and fire them at other people

and the main reason why is because this approach to things is part of the tradition that gets passed on from generation to generation

maybe not consciously or deliberately - but passed on nonetheless

when you live in a society where it is the norm for people to take their shit out on other people - odds are you wont find it hard to justify taking your shit out on other people yourself

in reference to the original shrapnel ideas - im gonna also propose that the 'positive' shrapnel is NOT ALWAYS accidental

i know some people that when they go thru foul shit - they reach for the pen

and the bomb they assemble is MEANT to turn that negative situation into something that people can touch / feel / use

at the very least - for me personally - when the difficulty of situations gets amped up - when im catching too much of the bullshit shrapnel - i seek to re-affirm the alliances i have made in the past and touch base with my foundation

in the process i benefit and look to approach the situation in ways that others can benefit as well

you can only build a brick shit house if you shit your hate properly

Thoughts on Shrapnel

BY PAYNE

Once upon a time, a little baby was born. There is nothing remarkable about this event - I'm told it happens every day - and there was nothing remarkable about this baby, except that it was you, or me, or them.

This baby was pristine, a sponge for information and experience. Little though it was, it was growing rapidly and learning every thing it could, as fast as it could. It had to, you see, because it's a big bad old world out there.

Everything the baby learned chipped a little bit of its personality away, or maybe it added a bit to it. This occured with every packet of information, every experience that came the baby's way. It was much like that saying about sculptors "freeing the statue" from the crude stone its encased in. Except that the sculptor is blind, like that woman in the Lionel Richie video (hah! "Hello, is it me you're looking for?!" except she's blind...), but I digress.

The tools that are used to "sculpt" this baby into the badass human that will stride the earth on two hind legs, using it's opposable thumbs like it just doesn't care, is what I call shrapnel.

It's when you are told about God. It's when you fall in love for the first time. It's when you realise, as a baby, that bawling your head off will have your mother
come running.

It's the "ripples" of things that happened long ago but that are still affecting us today. The shrapnel thrown out by history causes us to throw out our own shrapnel into the future. It blows your mind, it really does.

Shrapnel is necessary, and vital, to who we are and to what we do. And for Discordians, it can also be a tool. It's another medium for spreading a little bit of chaos. It's not "good" or "bad", though you may want to assess which bits of it you have sticking in you that aren't really needed. Unwatched, that shit can fuck you up.

In conclusion, Shrapnel is an idea that has yet to find its time. In the right hands, it can be a kick ass suit of armour AND a big-fuck-off flamethrower. For me, being aware of it is enough until some wiser heads can show us how it works.

Okay, I'm done preaching at you for now, I'm back off to my ivory tower, where I'll probably look for that Lionel Richie video and laugh about it all night.

THE GENTLE COWS STAND QUIETLY TO BE MILKED.

THE INFILTRATION OF THE INTERNET

The Internet is the most significant development in the evolution of human civilization since the printing press. The Printing press increased the communicative power of the individual. The internet gives the individual INFINITE potential for power of communication. The Net will become the storehouse of all human knowledge and history. It will become out immortal memory, and our second brain. (Good cause my first one isn't working too well, stupid blue screens). The Net is the soil in which our future will grow.

DON'T LET THEM HAVE CONTROL OF

The Net is the Sacred HIgh Seas of our world; The last bastion of true free range anarchy. Like the pirate seas of old, it is under constant attack by Greyface and his anal-retentive phalanx of Order-Mongers. Tjese attacks come in the form of Anti-Pornography Bills, corporate copyright lawsuits and the corruption of software companies, usally with money. The aim of this campaign is to stifle the Internet in it's infancy and forever reign it under the callous thumb of those currently in power; Greyface and the Lot.

NOW IS THE TIME TO FIGHT!

You can be part of the Immortal Battle! If you wish, you can make it your SACRED DUTY AND OBLIGATION TO FIGHT THE FORCES OF TYRANNY AND OPPRESSION to fight the forces of Dark Helmet's tyranny and oppression on the great frontier that is the net. We will applaud you. If we win, we will se a future flooded with the light of FREE INFORMATION and STFU TROLL. The hoarders; the Info-Lords, will be out of a job and forced to work for a living. Copyright laws will evaporate and the artists of the world will find themselves at the total mercy of their public. So they better behave themselves.

Did you know that one of the Old time Piracy's favorite ventures was freeing slave ships? Many of the freed slaves joined on as pirates and saved further ships.

"BUT WHAT IF I GET CAUGHT?"
MOTHERFUCKER YOU ARE ALREADY CAUGHT.
BETTER ASK YOURSELF: WHAT IF I GET FREE?

Whether or not you choose to acknowledge it, the world in which we live is abundant in absurdity. Sometimes, when day-to-day life becomes too methodic, and too predictable, people find themselves tuning out the weirdness, and passively continuing on around it. Some, have never even noticed the elephant in society's living room; that in our lives which is strange. Others thrive on the absurd, but are starved for it. They find themselves alienated, freaks in a society of complacent zombies.

As a Discordian of mind and of spirit, I have long felt a personal obligation to highlight the weirdness in the world around me. A few years ago, I was swimming in a lake, when a man in a full three-piece suit pulled up along the water and stepped out of his car. Casually, without removing his shoes or any of his clothing, he walked into the water until it was up to his neck. He turned towards me, and explained, "I do this every day." He shrugged, walked out of the water, and drove away, soaking wet. The man revealed to me something strange that I hadn't seen before. It threw me out of my own box and inspired me to stop hiding my own weirdness from those around me. Knowing that there were others out there, other freaks, other casual promoters of the strange, I exhaled.

Over the years, I've met many others who like me, share the same desire to facilitate discord. In early 2008, a call to action was launched, urging Discordians and the like to team up and work as a community on projects geared toward this sort of promotion. The ongoing project is called "OMGASM", or Operation: Mindfuck - Golden Apple Seed Missions. Here's how you play: anyone can create a Golden Apple Seed Mission, or a GASM. Once a GASM is created, (and promoted), networks of Discordians can join in on the fun simultaneously run with the mission. We're looking to throw people out of their boxes, to surprise them with unpredictability, to force them to confront what they may not understand, and let other freaks know that we're out there, pranking, laughing, and making the strangeness of this world a bit more overt. Having a team of people working towards a goal allows for large-scale mindfucks, and so far, the OMGASM project has delivered quite well.

"Colbertgasm" consisted of a mass snail mail letter writing campaign to TV personality Stephen Colbert, inviting him into the Bavarian Illuminati. To accept the invitation, Colbert was instructed to say certain code words on the air. Letters poured in from all over the world. Shortly after the project's letter writing week, Colbert casually uttered a code word, "23 skidoo", in the middle of an interview. He said it slowly, leaning in to the camera a bit. Those involved with Colbert Mission knew that they'd accomplished their goal. Though this in-joke was invisible to outsiders, the Discordian Society had worked together to create it. We had established an in-joke between our secret society and one of our mascots. Colbert is on our side. The OMGASM Network worked.

"Postergasm" is another example of a game that anyone can play. The mission is to hang up posters in cities, buildings, or anywhere where they will be seen. The project website states the objective: "Modify your environment. Reclaim public spaces. Surprise people out of their daily rut. Encourage creative thought." The posters may include images, single-sentence ideas, general nonsense, or anything else that can serve to throw your average person out of their pedestrian robot mode and announce to the community that weirdness lives. Some of the posters are funny, some serious, and others are downright nonsensical. The message can include whatever the person hanging the poster desires. This is an easy and fun mission, which can be played literally anywhere in the world.

The best thing about the project is that anyone can start a Golden Apple Seed Mission and invite others around the world to play along. Using the magic of the web, you can search for magic words like "OMGASM" and "Golden Apple Seed Mission" and find others who want help with their projects. This allows a great opportunity for Discordians everywhere to collaborate, and to go out and do something fun and strange. This is the information age. We now have the ability to play together, and really shake shit up. Need more chaos in your everyday? OMGASM is giving you the opportunity to make it happen..

Go ahead, start something big.

PROTIP *After you put up a poster, take a picture of it, upload it to flickr.com, and tag it "POSTERGASM". This will help encourage others to do the same.*

The Book of Dewlap

Zarathud the Confused Sage was speaking with his companions during teatime (being an American, who was in America at that time, this meant he was having tea at the proper, Greenwich Mean Time when it was the middle of the working day according to his local time zone. It made no difference), when one of them asked a question of him:

"Zarathud, the conundrum that we know as the 'Chicken or the egg' argument has vexed me lately. Which came first?"

Sipping his tea, Zarathud realized too late that the tea was very hot, and he proceeded to burn his tongue. Unable to answer the question, he waved his hand in an attempt to get another to speak for him.

Rising to meet the Confused and now Slightly Burned Sage's needs, a perceptive young companion spoke aloud: "What Zarathud means to say is that neither the chicken nor the egg seems to give a damn which came first, so we may conclude that they were born, simultaneously, from a potato bug."

Satisfied, Zarathud shrugged and those present were enlightened.

IN THE KINETIC ENERGY OF A MOVING FIST LIES A BIRTH-MACHINE FOR A PARALLEL UNIVERSE

Tips on Launching a Golden Apple Seed Mission

So you've got an idea for a jake or prank or project, and you want help. Here are some tips to make your idea take off:

- ☞ Keep it simple. If your GASM can't be explained in a paragraph or two, most people won't have the attention to follow.
- ☞ Make it FUN. Participation in the Mission should be rewarding in of itself. In fact, it should be fun even if you're not a Discordian
- ☞ Make it easy for people to participate. Don't make people generate their own material or do their own research. Make it Discordianproof.
- ☞ Expect to do most of the work yourself. Sad fact: It's not enough to build the funwagon, you've got to drive it too. Sometimes this will involve pushing it through mud and rain and harpies towards Funtown.
- ☞ LEADERSHIP and PERSISTENCE are perhaps the most important parts of starting a GASM. This project will quickly fizzle and die unless we have people THINKING FORWARD and LEADING BY EXAMPLE. This is YOUR opportunity to lead the pack into the wilderness. Don't get discouraged if your ideas don't take off immediately. It may take 5 or 10 false starts before you hit kallisti gold.
- ☞ ADVERTISE. Go push your idea at multiple Discordian locations. Also use digg, StumbleUpon, Facebook, and other popular web applications to broadcast your message to the masses. If you don't have accounts at these places, go make one. It's quick, and it increases your freedom to influence the Greater Network.

By the way, this article is a part of GASMGASM, the mission to spread the word about OMGASM. By the way, the last sentence is a part of GASMGASMGASM, the mission to spread the word about GASMGASM. By the way, the last sentence is a part of GASMGASMGASMGASM, the mission to never, ever STFU.

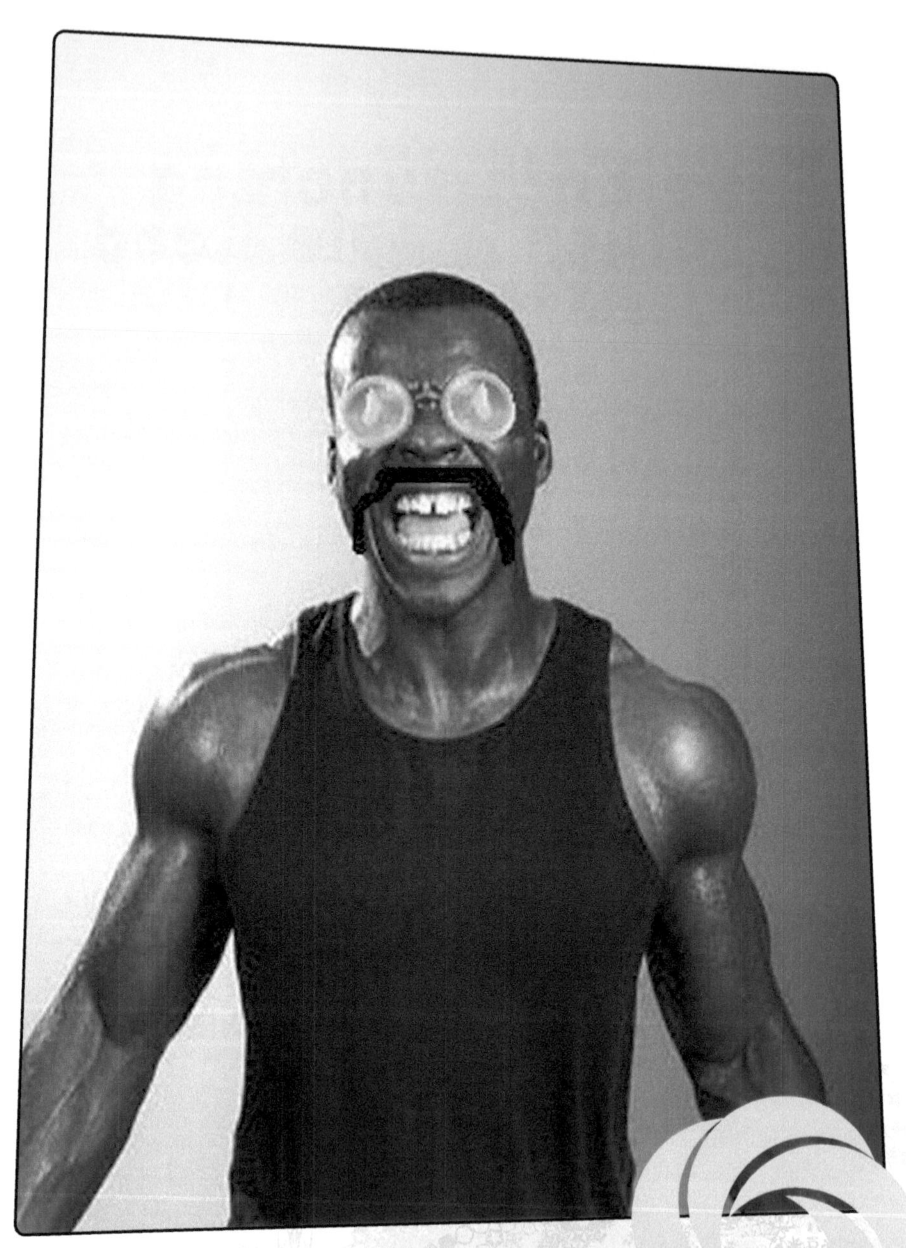

WHO CHOSE THE SCENERY?
WHO COMES UP WITH THE PLAYS?
WHO IS THE WRITER
WHO IS THE DIRECTOR?
WHO IS THE ACTOR?
WHO IS THE CAMERA?

Street Time

A cutup of Street Sermon (by DirtyEssence) and Save Money, Kill Time. Kill Money, Save Time (by FullTimeSlacker) and editing by Zarathud.

I'd like to begin with thanking you for taking this step, it means a lot to me to know that there are other people out there who look for the strange, the new. I've found a lot of many people's time is wrapped up in making sure they have enough money to weather the next shitstorm. The car breaks down, the kid breaks a leg, or the spouse breaks the bad news that she's leaving and taking half of everything and all of your dignity. . I know you paid for it and all, changed the oil every 3,000 miles and unfailingly paid the tolls, if you decide that you want to scratch off the VIN number the local man in blue can impound your car. Your gas gauge never gets above a half-tank on a good day. . Look, let's say you own a house built by your father's own two hands, and the house is built on land that was tamed by your great-great grandparents (the car that doesn't even drive anymore) a few centuries ago. Even if you have the deed in your hand, and even if you have not taken out any mortgages on the house, both house and land will be taken away from you if you fail to pay the property tax. You can hardly buy anything without credit, you need to have credit to get it.

I'm sorry to break it to you friend, but you do not own your own body . Of course, you can't STOP spending, especially on the things that make you feel happy. Look, if you decided you wanted to put a little stimulant in your body, you will have no job or benefits. Your sexual organs must keep quiet, because that is a severe legal offence. Gotta cram in one more hour of teevee, I know it's 1 AM, but I can get by on just 5 hours of sleep, right? I'll just poison myself into alertness. This is what I'm getting at friend. I believe that neither of us own our minds.

The harder you work to earn your money the less you get to enjoy it. The less you work the less you make, but you have a lot of time on your hands to worry about how much you don't have, right?

Fuck that.

See, what we call our ideas are mostly experiences we have had bubbling through our 5 senses or an expression of some relation between these experiences. They simply cannot own this, unless you decide to give it to them.

Work just the bare minimum, cut corners by re-using stuff as often as possible, grow some of your own food, and spend all of your money on marijuana so the official economy doesn't get any of it.

It is our last bastion of freedom, and certainly the most powerful tool we could ever possess. Look, I choose to believe that liberty is of nearly inexpressible value. This is certainly something that the powers that be want to portray. But when they use the term to what definition are they referring: the liberty of the individual or the liberty of the People? While away the blissful hours with a hobby that makes you happy and doesn't cost a lot. There is a difference. Everybody knows what it is like to experience something meaningful, everybody knows what it is like to have a happy experience. There's got to be something out there for you. When an object comes on the market it will certainly try to sell you on one or both of these aspects. You keep rushing back and forth hoping one day you'll have enough to stop working. This is where it all comes together.

You have already taken the first step in the process. I have not told you anything you did not already know, except this: there are people out there who truly want to you think critically not because they want to you follow their agenda or buy their product. If you did think critically what could we possibly convince you to do?

Myspace Monkeys

If you are here looking for frivolous material, obscene content, or anything that the enemy has put out in the name of Discordianism in order to obfuscate, then you are in the wrong place. The enemy has blinded the world to the true face of Eris by turning Discordianism into a joke. Read on if you aren't happy with ignorance, as they would like you to be. —ROBO

Stack! is a discordian game the concept of which has been reached independently by the whimsical and the mystical and the shenanigan-loving. the basic idea is that of putting things on top of other things. The picture i put up for my face shot or whatever that's supposed to be is an example of Stack! produced by myself and Mr. Kade Johnson at Bentley college one day. It is 20 chairs, stuck in the most precarious formation possible into a ghastly yet amazingly aesthetic, mostly random shape, entirely balanced on top of a single chair in the usual position for chairs (with four legs on the ground).

why is Stack! such a sweet game, and why is it discordian you ask? allow me to explain, and thank you for asking those questions. Stack! exhibits the concepts of order and chaos intertwined and of the ever present precarious balance. during the course of Stack! objects are stacked one at a time in the least stable positions possible (many of the chairs in the picture are supported by a single leg standing on a seat, and similar improbable structures). when objects are placed atop the unstable objects, the weight of the new objects secures them slightly. the random, spur of the moment placement of objects in precarious balance produces a structure of relative stability in the end, locking tightly as it becomes more chaotic, developing a certain order out of its chaos.

so that's Stack! tell your friends! it's a metric pantload of fun, and i reccomend try it out.

tern facilitates control over the other(s), depending (among other factors) upon the number of common elements involved.

Why is there no laughter in the Bible? Why doesn't Yahweh Himself, human-all-too... step up to the joke and show His love by unloading ... the harried, overstressed Israelites? ... seems to be a distinctly new sobriety at work in the ancient Judaic desert cult that burgeoned into Christianity. (Compare with polytheism's raring array of tricksters, jokes, pranks, and confidence-games) Is this phenomenon related to Plato's banishing of the poets in The Republic? Is comedy a Satanic principle of diffusion and a reckless toying with the holy source code of Universal Truth?

quite funny. You just don't understand his sense of humor. I mean come on, "the meek shall inherit the earth," right Jesus,

(from page 62) greatest insult comedian of his generation. text below might belong to Schizo Testament or not

BRUNETTI II-1 "You know what the problem is? My philosophy's been GONADECTOMIZED. I did NOT

after finding out that the semi-false holiday was really about getting together part of a consensus reality) and yet still be true provided it works in a specific situation."

"LAW OF PRAGMATISM If a pattern of belief or behavior enables a being to survive and to accomplish chosen goals, then that belief or behavior is true, realistic, and/or sensible."

"LAW OF FINITE SENSES Every sense mechanism of every entity is limited by both range and type of data perceived, and many real phenomena exist which may be outside the sensory scanning ability of any given entity."

"LAW OF ASSOCIATION if any two or more patterns have elements in common, the patterns interact "through" those common elements. The control of one pattern facilitates control over the other(s), depending (among other factors) upon the number of common elements involved."

Why is there no laughter in the Bible? Why doesn't Christ ever crack a joke? Why doesn't Yahweh Himself, human-all-too-human that He is, ever step up to the mike and show His love by unloading a side-splitting zinger or two on the harried, overstressed Israelites? There seems to be a deadly new sobriety at work in the ancient Judaic desert cults that burgeoned into Christianity. (Compare with polytheism's dazzling array of tricksterism, jokes, pranks, and confidence games.) Is this phenomenon related to Plato's banishing of the poets in The Republic? Is comedy a Satanic principle of diffusion and a reckless toying with the holy source-code of Universal Truth?

maybe he was quite funny and you just don't understand his sense of humor, i mean come on, "the meek shall inherit the earth." right Jesus, ahhahaha, that's priceless. maybe the whole Son of God thing was one huge practical joke designed to get him crucified, thus fulfilling the Hebrew prophecy through his blasphemy, and sparking the religion that would dominate the world for the next 2000 years. joke's on us i guess...

"PEOPLE ARE KEEPING AND EXCLUSIVELY GIVING LOVE TO ONE PERSON! IT MUST BE A JOKE! WELL, EH ... THAT'S THE THING ... IT IS. DO YOU HAVE ANY IDEA HOW COMMON CHEATING REALLY IS? BUT COMMON PEOPLE LIKE TO PRETEND" - DR STRANGELOVE OR HOW I LEARNED TO STOP WORRYING AND LOVE THE BOMB

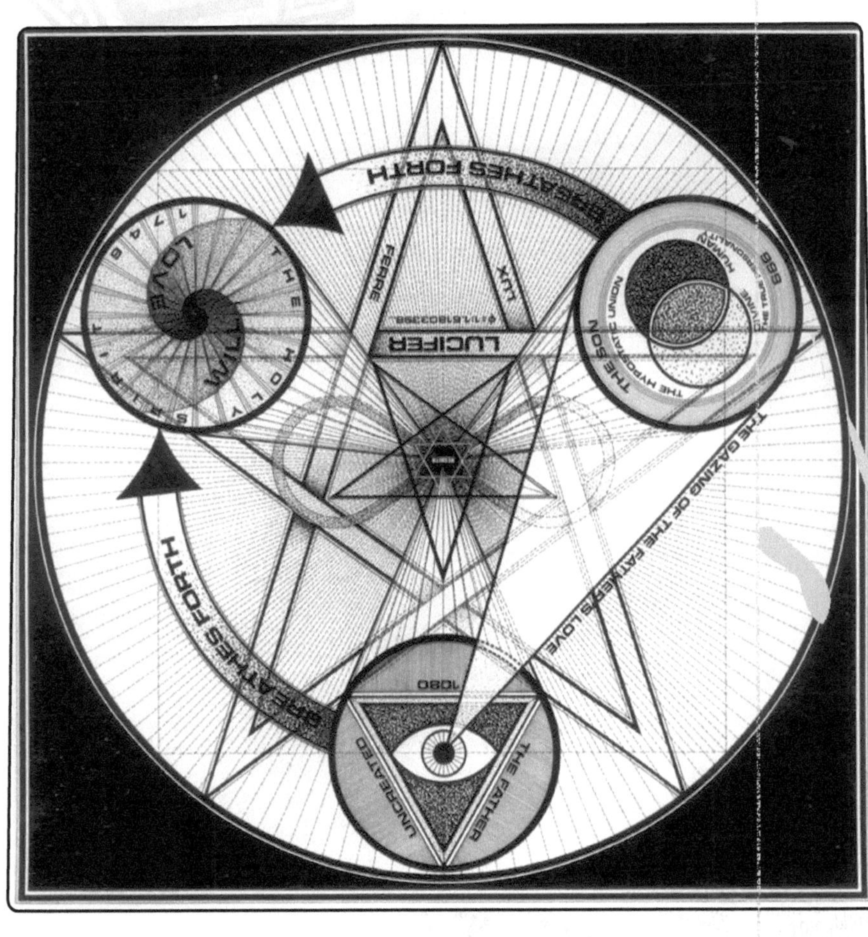

It's a little known idea in some circles of learning that Christ was in fact the greatest insult comedian of his generation. text below might belong to Schizo Testament or not

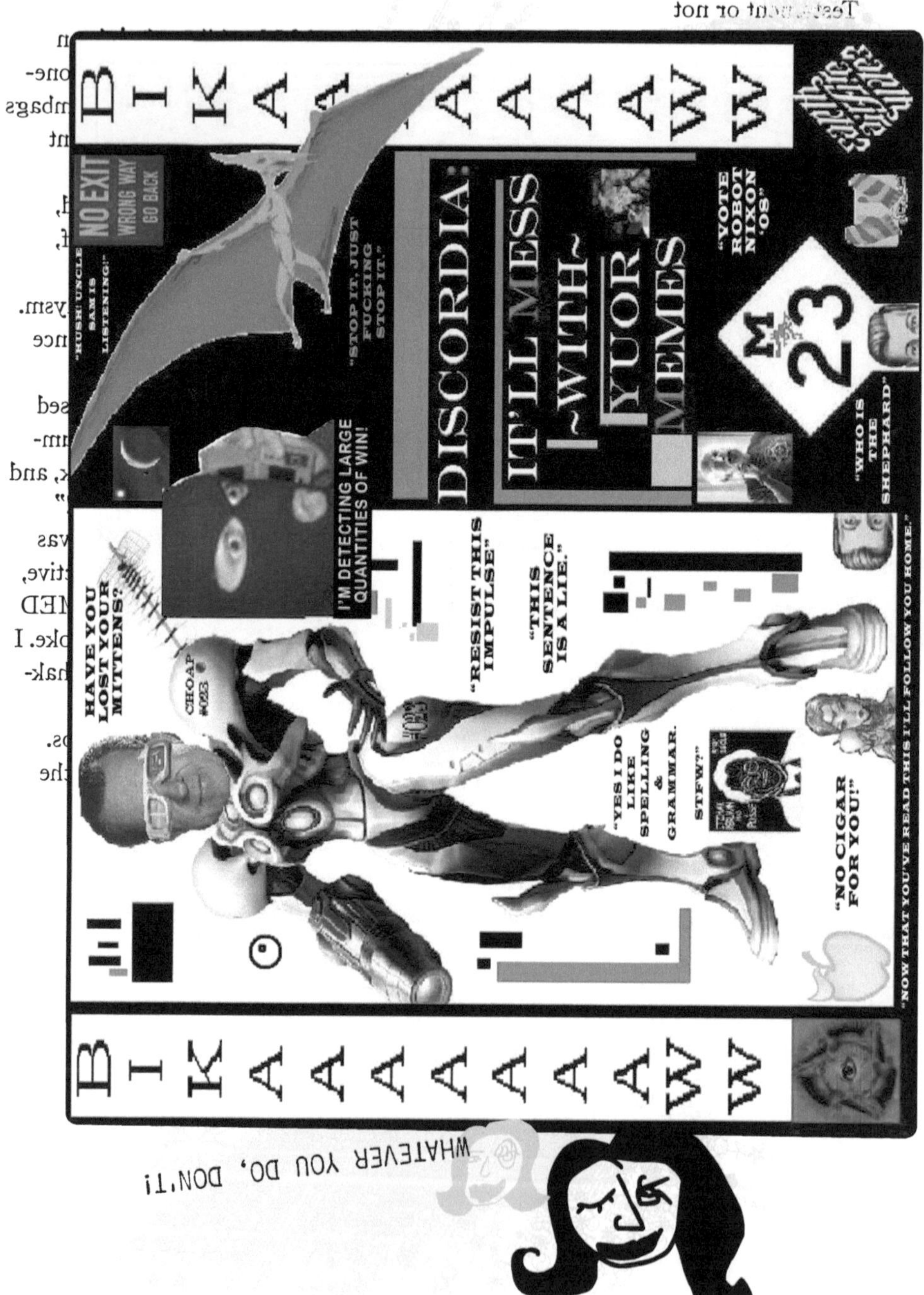

WHATEVER YOU DO, DON'T!

A disciple entirely sick of normal teachings sought enlightenment at the foot of a self proclaimed master. Meeting the master at a park bench, the student heeded the words of a hand lettered sign on a disused case of beer, and handed $40.00 to the holy one.

"Let me ask you this:", began the student, feeling now entitled to a certain lesson.

"No.", replied the master, as he tucked away the bills.

"Yes, but my questions is...", he began again.

"It isn't. You fool youself.", came the reply.

"I ONLY WISH TO ASK ONE THING!" the disciple bellowed, now feeling quite fed up.

"You have asked three things, and have a lesson for today. Go and ponder this."

Once his blood pressure fell, feeling quite humbled, the student bowed and left, pondering what had occured. As he left he saw another fellow approach the master cashless, greeting him affably and sharing a certain brown wrapped drink. Seeing this, the student went off, feeling there was much indeed to think on.

A Zen Master went to visit a Discordian KSC high upon a mountain top.

The Zen Master carefully approached the Discordian, being aware of their erratic temperment. Before he could speak, the Discordian spun around and asked the Zen Master, "Does the Goddess Eris have Buddha-Nature?"

The Zen Master smiled and said, "Mu!"

The Discordian looked the Zen Master in the eyes and said, "What the fuck is that supposed to mean?"

The Zen Master smiled and said, "Mu!"

The Discordian stood and said, "No, man. I'm serious. What the fuck does that mean? Are you retarded or something?"

The Zen Master smiled and said, "Mu!"

The Discordian snatched the Zen Master's walking stick away from him and said, raising his voice, "Say 'Mu' Again. Say 'Mu' again. I dare you. I double-dare you, motherfucker! Say 'Mu' one more God Damn time!"

The Zen Master was no longer smiling, but was holding up his shaking hands defensively and said, "Mu?"

The Discordian moved closer, savagely striking the Zen Master with his own stick, all the time shouting, "Is the Goddess Eris a beautiful blonde with big tits and an ass that tastes like French vanilla ice cream? Answer me!"

When the Zen Master awoke, he found that his wallet was gone and his pineal gland was swollen. He also noticed that his underwear was on inside-out.

LORD OMAR'S PICK-UP TRUCK

A blonde bodacious student of Discordia asked Lord Omar, "Your place or my place?" Lord Omar asked, "Are you on the pill?" The blonde bodacious student answered, "Yes, I am." Lord Omar said, "Then fuck it! I can't hold it any longer, let's do it here on the hood of my truck."

BY IGNATIOUS DRYROASTED CHAFFINCH

Pope Joan was said to have been the first lady in England to take on the call of the Discordi. It is told in The Honest Book Of Truth that most sacred of Discordian tomes, that Eris came to her when she was but 16 years old.

"H.B.O.T Chapter 0, Verse 12: And as Joan Dearborne Smythe was cleaning out the privy, there was a blinding flash of purple light and a woman appeared unto her clothed all in gold. Joan did drop to her knees and did cry out 'Oh strange spirit, do not hex me, for I am but a lowly sheep farmers daughter, and know not of the doings of the other world.'

The strange woman did grin and spake in a voice dripping with honey: 'Fear not gentle Joan, for I have come to give unto thee the secrets of the multiverse. You shall know why it is that toasted bread always falls butter side down, how it is that it is always thee left sock that vanishes upon wash day, why it always rains when you go to the seaside and the mystery of the twenty and three.' And unto Joan did this strange woman render an apple of purest gold and again did spake again:

'Here is my Graile Discordia, meditate upon this and the entire truth and wisdom of the teachings of The Discordi will be yours. Not to mention this excellent set of crystal tumblers and these fine steak knives.'

And the strange woman did vanish, leaving her apple of purest gold sat on the corner of the privy. And for twenty and three days did Joan meditate upon the secrets of the apple.

Upon doing this, she was enlightened, and received the Wholley Wisdom Of Eris.

After receiving Eris in the privy, Joan did take the title of Pope Joan The First, and she set out to wander the lands of England, spreading the secret wisdom of Eris.

It is said that using only a wiffle stick and a salted mackerel, Pope Joan did drive all of the Fnords out of England. It is self evident that she succeeded in this, as there is not a single Fnord to be seen, nowadays in the UK.

Pope Joan was the first Discordian to consider the power of the Pineal Gland. In her Sermon To Thee Hounds, which she preached to the Count Of Basingstoke's hunting pack, she makes mention of it:

"And if thy feels a tingle in thy gland of thee pineal, one must open it wide, and stroke it. Even thou art lowly hounds one may see thee anerisistic confusion of thee grey reality. Chase thy tails and lick thy balls, oh hairy brethren, and fall ye not into presets of order."

Pope Joan wandered England during a period from 830 AD till 845 AD, converting random strangers, and preaching to house pets, till circumstances forced her into hiding.

It is said that after she received the Graile, she was hunted out by the forces of The Grey Order.

By an amazing stroke of lateral thinking, Pope Joan worked out that if indeed she was being hunted out, and that, in fact the hunters were looking for a female Discordian Pope, that the best place to hide would be within the catholic Clergy.

In a reverse echo of the film Nuns On The Run 17, Pope Joan Cut her hair, bound up her lady chests and assumed the guise of a Franciscan Monk.

Indeed this disguise proved to be rather too successful. Through no doing of her own, the young monk John (as she cunningly changed her name to), rose through the ranks of clergy and in 854 AD was tenured with becoming the Catholic Pope.

Joan was rightfully amused at this prospect and decided that she could use this interesting turn of circumstance to sew the seeds of Discord into the very center of the Roman Catholic Church.

Things went well for Pope John / Joan for quite some time until around 857 AD when according to legend, whilst in transit from the Colosseum to the Church of San Clemente, Pope John / Joan gave birth to a son, whilst dressed in full pontifical gear. No doubt this was a bit of a shock to those cardinals traveling with him / her, and it seemed to be a bit of a shock to Pope Joan also, as she died on the spot.

Ever since then, the Vatican has insisted that any prospective popes, visit St John Lateran. In this chapel one will find a blood red marble chair, with a hole in the seat. This has been used ever since to check out the sex of prospective popes, so as to avoid any further Jonarian style confusion.

As we can see from the passage taken from The Honest Book Of Truth Pope Joan was in position of the Graile Discordia. After her untimely death, we can only assume that it was taken to the Vatican for safe keeping. With the Graile Discordia being kept hushed up by the powers at the Vatican, there is not much known about these Dark Ages Of Discordia, rumor has it that Eris herself was rightfully miffed at having her apple swiped and took it out on the Mayans. This, however cannot be proved.

With the teachings of Pope Joan still circulating the word of Discordia could not be hushed up. In 1123, a renegade group of knights formed a splinter group to continue the works of Eris. These brave knights named themselves The Knights Hemplar, a derivative of the original organization The Knights Templar, who as you may not be aware existed as a military arm of The Grey Conspiracy, dedicated to stamping out Erisine teachings, and keeping the secret of The Graile Discordia from the masses.

ATTRACTION AND DISTRACTION KEEPS THINGS IN YOUR DREAM (LOVE AND HATE ETC). BY ACCEPTING THINGS THEY PASS ON, NOT ACCEPTING TEND TO MAKE THEM COME BACK UNTIL ACCEPTED OR DEALT WITH. DON'T ACCEPT THE UNACCEPTABLE.

The Parable of Steve

BY NIGEL

There was an afternoon one summer when a young man we will call "Steve" happened upon a book like no other he had read. It was on the shelf in his local alternative bookstore, and it was called the "Principia Discordia".

Steve had always thought himself to be quite the rebellious young man, always speaking out about the Man and the System, but with a sense of HUMOR, goddamnit, a sense of ABSURDITY unlike everyone else he knew; this book, he said to himself, is Important. It finally tells me what I am…I am a Discordian. I must find the others!

It took Steve some time to find other Discordians, time during which he renamed himself Pope Buttercup XXIII. He felt that quite a fitting name for a Discordian. He prided himself in his sense of Absurdity, and especially his skills in Randomness, which he practiced by memorizing passages from the Principia.

He learned on the Internet that the Discordian Society near him met monthly in a café downtown, and after his months of searching he determined the date and the time, and arranged to present himself to them. When he arrived, he found the place nearly deserted except for a group of ten or twelve people clustered in a back corner, arguing. They were of all descriptions, these people; no two seemed to have anything in common, even their styles of dress; they ranged from the glowering pierced goth chick at one corner, who was seated beside a neatly-groomed silver-haired man in a rather nice suit, to the plump middle-aged matron in a V-necked rayon sweater, to the lively trenchcoat geek thumping his opinion about something-or-other loudly in the middle of the table.

Steve said to himself, "These are my people?"

"What a motley crew… well, they're Discordians, I know how to show them I'm One Of Them."

He stepped up to the table.

"23PINEALFNORD!" he said boldly, "I am Pope Buttercup XXIII! I am random, and say randomly absurd things, because I am a Discordian like you!"

The group fell silent and looked at him curiously for a moment, and then resumed arguing.

Steve was puzzled. This wasn't the reception he'd expected. He spoke again;

"Excuse me, but do you know where the monkeys fly at midnight? Modern politics bores me, and I can swallow my own nose!!"

Now a few of the others seemed to be paying attention to him, although to his dismay they seemed less than impressed by his perfect grasp of outlandishness. Two or three of them, he noticed... why, they were making fun of him! They were whispering to each other, and looking at him, and laughing! He flushed red in anger.

"Listen, you people! I am a Discordian, and I know what Discordia is, and I came here to find Answers and Truth and Nonsense and Absurdity... what do I find you doing? Just... NOTHING! Nothing at all! Why aren't you Saying Important Nonsense? Why, you're just ARGUING... ARGUING like any schmucks I might find on the street! I am obviously more enlightened and Discordian than you fools. You people are all just alike. You should be different! You should PAY ATTENTION to ME, and LISTEN to ME, and I will show YOU How to Be Discordian!"

With this, he started dancing and squawking around the table like a big, Steve-shaped chicken, periodically uttering Absurdities such as "I AM THE PAULRUS" and "TOGETHER WE TURNTABLE THE GREEN OTTER!". The people at the table attempted to carry on with their arguing, but it was getting harder and harder to hear each other over the squawking. Soon, all their arguing was about Steve, and whether they should ask him to leave. About a third of the group started shouting at Steve, telling him to get out of the café and leave them alone; another third started shouting at the first third to shut up and leave Steve alone, and the other third tried to have an interesting conversation, but it was impossible to follow with all the hubbub so they eventually fell silent.

Finally, the barista stormed over and said, "WHAT IN THE HELL IS GOING ON OVER HERE?"

One of the quieter members of the group replied, "Discord".

We would like, at this point, to say that Steve, hearing this, was enlightened, but it doesn't usually work that way outside of Zen koans.

I have a little brown messenger bag which waits by the door for me like a puppy wanting to go out. In my bag, I carry a few pages of stickers, some markers, post-it notes, pope cards, my notebook, a camera, two fake moustaches, and a folder containing a few hundred posters. I like to walk around the neighborhood, putting up flyers, making changes to signs, and generally jaking around.

One day, past midnight, a one-eyed bum approached me on the street. "What've ya got there?" he asked. "I seen your pictures around the neighborhood. What ARE you doing?" I blinked. This question always stumps me. It's a funtime activity I've never really attached a name to other than "putting up stuff".

Searching my brain for a quick explanation, I eventually told him, "It's art," but the word stuck in my throat. Well I guess you could argue that anything is art,
certainly some of the stuff I put up is artistic, but I don't really consider this activity art.

I lay in bed that night, the question turning over in my mind:

What AM I doing?

For one, I'm taking back my environment and gradually transforming it into the place I want it to look like. I like making everybody's day a little bit more surreal, and this is a really visible way of doing it.

For two, I know that somewhere out there, there are other people like me. Other people who appreciate these weird little intrusions into pedestrian reality. My posters are signposts saying "I'm here, and you're not alone."

And for three, it sends the message to everyone that public spaces are public property. We all modify our environment by living in it. The sounds and smells and rhythms of the neighborhood are an organic reflection of its occupants.

Putting up posters is just like trimming the hedges or mowing the lawn.

Walking through the neighborhood with my bag over my shoulder, my cabal at my side, I'm reminded of don Juan Matus and Carlos Castaneda on their way to Ixtlan, trying to walk with the entities and intelligences of the desert. We're urban shamans, befriending the spirit of the neighborhood. While you go on your ventures, I reccommend this attitude, one of respect and stewardship for your environment, your companion on this journey.

I've been regularly putting up posters in this neighborhood for about a year now, and I think it's "working". At first, they'd dissapear quickly, but they're staying up much longer now. I think people are either laughing at them (and leaving them up) or are getting tired of taking them down. I like the fact that when I walk from point A to point B, I get to chuckle at the cool stuff hung on the telephone poles, walls, and trees, the moustaches drawn on posters, the stickers in the phonebooths. It feels like MY neighborhood. I am having such a blast doing this, I can only hope that somebody else out there is digging it half as much as I am.

I don't have any agenda higher than that. That's why I tend to avoid posters with political or ideological propaganda on them - people have a lot of defense mechanisms when they sense someone's trying to sell them something. I just want them to stop for a second and be aware of their environment. I want to jolt them, if only briefly, out of their pedestrian autopilot. And after seeing a few hudred of these signs, maybe they'll join me in modifying their environment for the better. Or maybe when they realize how easy it is to have fun FOR YOURSELF, IN YOUR OWN WAY, they'll loosen up, just a bit.

If you want to join me, but you're stuck for ideas for what to put up, search the web for our code word, PosterGASM. I've collected quite a bit of material over at http://www.blackironprison.com/index.php?title=POSTERGASM. I also advise you to take pictures of your work and post it on flickr.com with the tag "POSTERGASM". That way, you'll KNOW you're not out there alone. There's a community of people who also dig these kinds of shenanigans, and we love it when other pranksters choose to help carry the torch into the Strange Times.

May your stapler be full and your stickers be sticky. May your streets be filled with laughter. And may your posters hang high, long, and deep.

PICTURE ALL EVENTS, SCENES, MOMENTS IN LIFE stuffed on top of one another like the bricks in strange giant Tetris — all existing Now. Watch all the identities slowly moving upwards, and the puny changes they make in the Tetris by different choices and doings they do. A place where the I's (eyes) experience themselves and each other. Welcome to the Dream Theater!

PRINT A FEW COPIES GO FROM DOOR TO DOOR OFFER THE WORD OF LIES, TRUTH, DISORDER AND PLUMPER HOT DOGS

HELP ME

I HAVE AN ALIEN BRAIN VIRUS AND IT IS MAKING ME PUT UP THESE POSTERS. I CAN'T STOP. I HAVE NOT SLEPT FOR DAYS. PLEASE SOMEONE HELP ME. ZZWLETTZYLZTLTYTYTLZ

Oh, hello dear! What? That fapping noise just now? That was me. I was fapping.
Fap
u

The Cloved Lemon Kissing Game

BY PRINCESS UNICORNIA AND REVEREND LOVESHADE

This holy ritual was discovered by members of the Society for Creative Anachronism, which stubbornly insists it is not a division of the Ek-sen-triks CluborGuild. (The SCA was founded on the anniversary of the Bavarian Illuminati in 1966 in California, just one year after Principia Discordia was first published in California, which sounds mighty suspicious to us). The ritual has five steps, naturally.

1. Someone, the Lemon Clover, inserts cloves into a fresh lemon (or some other fruit, in which case this person is the Some Other Fruit Clover. But pucker-inducing lemons generally work best). Making a pattern with the cloves is optional. Possible patterns include a heart, smiley face, the number five, the Sacred Chao, or the Mormon Tabernacle Choir. It's generally best to prepare the lemon shortly before the game begins, although the cloved lemon can be refrigerated for a short while.
2. One person, the Giver, hands the cloved lemon to someone e would like to kiss, called the Receiver. Usually this is done at a party or other get-together, except funerals. The game generally happens while other things are going on, sometimes continuing through a whole party.
3. The Receiver then takes a clove out with es teeth to freshen es breath. If the Receiver doesn't like the taste of cloves, e may use es hand. If played in a hot tub, declare a non-breakable container to be the Sacred Used Clove Receptacle. If played anywhere else, a clove may be deposited wherever is appropriate, as swallowing cloves can be pretty nasty.
4. The Receiver indicates the body part the Giver may kiss by offering that body part to the Giver and/or pointing to it. Usual locations are the hand, cheek, lips, open mouth/tongue. Unusual locations are left to the imagination. However, the nature of the kiss should always be mutually agreeable. The Giver should be gracious, even if the kiss is less intimate than e desired.

5. The Receiver now becomes the Giver, and goes to Step 2. This continues until your lemon runs out of cloves (in which case you may either end the game or go to Step 1), or players run out of body parts. (But body parts, unlike cloves, are reusable. And rekissible.)

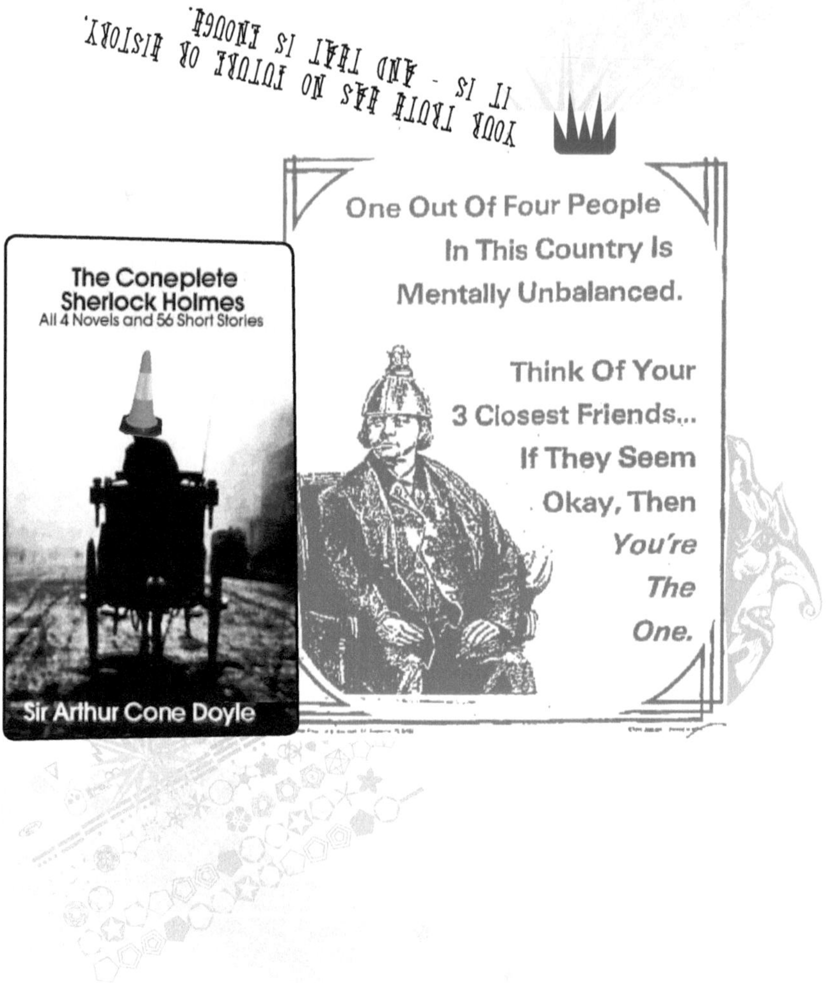

The Coneplete Sherlock Holmes
All 4 Novels and 56 Short Stories
Sir Arthur Cone Doyle

One Out Of Four People In This Country Is Mentally Unbalanced.

Think Of Your 3 Closest Friends... If They Seem Okay, Then *You're The One.*

The following message was channelled through Princess Madnonymus from the Shlok: Y'H-SH'RP-E-DU-DUDU-DEDA-DADA (THE CASTRATION OF THE SHLOK)

"My faith in its nature is not logical; Thus, then, my logic is not an immutable fact. My faith in its nature not being an immutable fact, I therefore say that it is circular and true."

"Lose sight of this principle of circumvolution and prefer to think in logical terms; You then obtain a view of things as either right or wrong but immutable. If afterwards you say that they are to be exchanged for currencies, You thus come to see things in a dogmatic and righteous way."

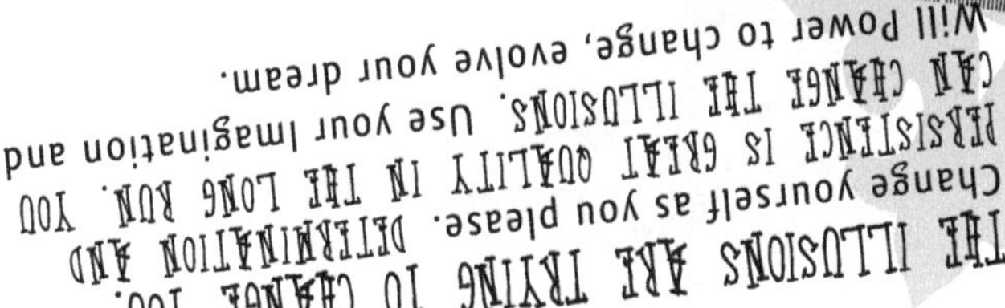

"EVERYONE IS THEIR OWN SOLUTION!
LET THE LOVE BE FREE..." - DR STRANGELOVE OR HOW
I LEARNED TO STOP WORRYING AND LOVE THE BOMB.

Hearts and Minds

Welcome to the modern day war zone. Right now, as I speak, a thousand battles are being waged for your submission and allegiance. Commanders and politicians have decided that the enemy is us and that we are to be bought to heel, as soon as possible.

No doubt some of you think I'm using hyperbole, or metaphor to illustrate an example of our socially fractured society and the commodification of identity. And while those certainly are problems, anyone thinking about those in relation to my rant today are wrong. Right now, you and I are quite literally at war with at least one government, namely that of the USA.

Oh to be sure there won't be running battles with light infantry. No air-strikes are going to be called in on your house, and I'm reasonably certain you wont get carted away to Guantanomo Bay, or any other black site that exists. But just because guns aren't being loaded and blood isn't been spilt doesn't mean this isn't a conflict.

You see, war isn't about the clash of armies on the battlefield anymore. Hell, its barely even about killing, except as an advertising hook or a final solution for people who refuse to stop being a pain in the ass. No, warfare has moved through the gentlemanly period of pitched battles and low casualties, blown apart by Napoleon and perfected in the slaughterhouse of WWI. Its not even the dirty political warfare that characterized the Cold War, marked by futile superpower conflict and strategies designed to bleed a superpower by third world proxies, and on the other end of the scale by terrorism.

No, warfare today is about fighting on the psychological and narrative level. Its about capturing the mind, and shackling it to the agenda of the day, regardless of what that agenda may be.

The thing is, you see, as warfare has become less and less about artful strategy and less bound by codes of conduct – be they religious, cultural or legal – the real issue has not been arms, logistics, intelligence and skill, but about the sheer will to fight. Whoever goes on fighting the longest, whoever is willing to do what it takes to persuade the other side to accept their interests, whoever is able to effectively frame the agenda in a certain manner, is the winner in the modern world. You can even suffer strategic setbacks if your message and will is powerful enough.

And of course, if you accept this as essentially true, broadly speaking, then logically you come to the problem being people who wont get the fuck on with the message. The enemy ceases to be those who threaten certain strategic alliances, deposits of raw materials and the lives of the citizenry. No, the enemy becomes anyone who undermines that message and so weakens that will to resolve the conflict – and that person can be anyone, even your own citizenry.

Back in the day, they used to call this PsyOps. It used to only be a wartime enterprise. Dropping leaflets over enemy cities and troop formations. Doing pirate broadcasts using exiles and friendlies from the nation you are at war with to convince them of widespread resentment towards the government. Smear and ridicule important political and military leaders in any way possible.

Like I said, it used to be only a wartime enterprise. But now, thanks to the Cold War terrorism, carried to its conclusion by the likes of Al-Qaeda and Hezbollah, the difference between peace and war only exists in a legal sense. The potentially endless war on terror means actually endless psychological operations – carried out against not just the enemy, but the civilian population at home as well. The media has to hang the enemy with words and discourses and justifications before the military can do it in fact.

Nowadays, PsyOps is only one part of a much broader school, known as Information Operations. Do you operate a blog, report on the failing and lies and crimes of your country? Then you are are, according to this world-view, engaging in warfare against the state. But its not just about information per se. You have to think about this much more broadly. For example, protests. A protest is not just a protest. It never can be. Its an expression of low intensity conflict relying on moral discourses and popular expression of dissidence, aimed at bringing about a political-military confrontation.

And just where do you think something like Operation MindFuck fits into this system of ideas? Since many of us tend to think of O:MF as a way of mentally shaking people up, getting them to question their assumptions, physically deconstructing the popular discourses of the day, stripping away the bare truth hidden beneath self-serving platitudes...well, in that case, it is nothing more than a direct challenge to state power.

That may dishearten some of you. But the simple truth is, thinking for yourself, and then communicating those thoughts to others, will always be seen that way, so long as this world-view dominates. You may as well get used to it, because unless you decide to never share your views, or have a frontal lobotomy, you will almost certainly do something that could be considered an act of war. And if you get really good at it, you may even end up in a real domestic war –

as the crazy elements of the thuggish far right, security services and corporate sponsored smear teams conspire to make your life hell through intimidation, surveillance and character assassination.

And to be honest, once you realize that you are in the war, a certain clarity accompanies that knowledge. You can now diagnose this uneasy feeling all of the above has been creating. You know what it is now, the nature of the Beast is discerned and laid bare. Once you know what the problem is, you can set about dealing with it. Few things are insurmountable, once you understand their purpose and context.

Unfortunately, you have little choice about this. The line has already been drawn in the sand, and you're on the wrong side. What happens next is a matter of policy, insanity, personal whim and plain old bad luck. Because you're not quite the perpetual pain in the ass that, say, Al-Qaeda is, you won't be facing the guns. You can be drowned out by voices of far-right harpies, military "experts" who 'just happen' to be taking pay cheques from the Pentagon and spineless journalists more content with attacking those who search for the truth than politicians who hide it.

There is a spectrum of responses, if you will. If you do this, the response will be that. And if you do something else, the response will differ in proportion. But like all Platonic constructs of reality, there are gaps in the conceptual definitions put forward. And it is in such gaps that the game must be played most effectively. Operation MindFuck works best in areas where they are no response. So go beyond blogging, or political protest, or pranks, or sabotage and mild acts of ontological guerilla warfare. Mix and match, be innovative, experiment and push the boundaries. And remember, even though this is a war, unconventional forces always have the advantage over hierarchies.

H E S I T A T I O N

IS FOR THOSE WHO CAN'T HANDLE THE IMPACT.

THE SANITY IS : IN

Divine Madness

In a nation of people who are moving to a morality based on xenophobia and arbitrary discrimination masked as ethical superiority, there exists a subculture of sinners, heretics and transgressors of the laws of the concrete jungle. These people, whether their existence be one of idyllic communion or of desperate nonconformity, become the pariahs of their progenitors, neither understood nor respected by their peers as they dance a mad dance that frightens the man on the street due to intensity, subtlety or sheer incomprehensibility. These individuals, being reflections of the nature of our possibility and our futility, frighten as well as remind the world of the dangers of excess as well as the draining wounds of its own banality. Those who are able to convince the world of the validity of their own mad prophecy become the icons of an era, while those without the requisite advertising skills rot in a cage of confusing expectations and near insanity. Only extreme options are available to those with the gift of Divine Madness. If you have a problem, if no one else can help, and if you can find them, maybe you can hire... The E-Team

Most of what consists of 'neo-paganism' is actually an eclectic mishmash of fairy tales, anthropological conjecture, New Age sensibilities and outright wishful thinking. There is no hard evidence that the 'witches' and 'pagans' that modern pagans cite had anything resembling the same moral sensibilities that we do. Real data about their lives is scarce or biased. Modern occult draws mostly from publicity-hungry writers like Crowley, modern interpretations of incomplete and dubious medieval sources and from the media. The modern pagan learns more about magick and religion from The Craft, Mercedes Lackey and Harry Potter than any kabbalistic, alchemical or hermetic source.

Those who continue to explore religious, spiritual and magickal issues tend to go from an eclectic Pop-paganism to an examination of established religious traditions. However, the quantity and variety of religious thought now available is staggering.

The major change in human interaction in the technological age has been the speed and ubiquity of communications. Cultures clash constantly as other cultural structures are exposed to (and impressed upon) the peoples of every culture and subculture. This exposure has led to a quasi-Darwinian 'survival of the most interesting' competition in American society in which ideologies are sampled like foods in a salad bar. The result is a theological consumerism where devout observance of a particular tradition is an unacceptable form of bigotry given the diversity of seemingly-devout experience available. Thus we have a pagan community with a sort of Deist agnosticism, taking what they can of each religious experience and gluing them together into a collage of spiritual belief to justify their nebulous sense of the existence of a divinity different from that of the accepted societal dogma.

That is not to say that the magick they do or the religious affinities they have are not real or as valid as the Deist agnosticism that passes for modern American Christianity. However, without a conscious understanding of the fact that modern pagan and occult sensibilities have bootstrapped themselves into existence instead of having imaginary connections to idealized ancient cultures, those sensibilities will continue to be a sort of spiritual masturbation. The unconscious appropriation of ideological icons does not provide any sort of understanding of original significance of those icons, nor does the individual have the requisite knowledge to integrate those concepts into any sort of useful framework. Without significant mindfulness, such Rube-Goldberg ideologies simply become idle curiosities, ciphers for mainstream morality or a cover for the pervasive amorphous belief in some divinity in some shape or form.

The above begs for the step of conscious appropriation in a post-modern manner. The confrontation with multiple cultural sensibilities and religious systems has indicated the existence of a wide variety of ways that life can be lived and interpreted. We have to deal with the fact that Modern Western Culture is not the evolutionary pinnacle of societal development. Our near-instantaneous global contact has shown us that there are an innumerable number of distinct cultures and sub-cultures out there that can and have produced viable communities and outlooks for their participants. With this surplus of data, the post-modern response is to divine the potential significance of these religious systems so that they can be duplicated in a framework of interlocking ideas that provides a unique whole. A techno or industrial musician samples sounds, baselines and words and remixes them into a new song reminiscent of many of the elements of the original parts yet having its own individual character. Similarly, the pomo-pagan combs the threads of spiritual and social experience for the building blocks and gears of a theological structure that utilizes the actualities and potentialities of the ancient, the popular and the possible as a metaphysical outlook that is in synch with the unique character of an inhabitant of the 21st century.

"ALL THAT WAS: WILL BE. ALL THAT WASN'T: CAN'T. NOW FETCH ME A POP TART MOTHERFUCKER." —COLIN POWELL IN ONE OF HIS MORE LUCID MOMENTS.

A lot of modern paganism is progressing towards this state. A large number of new adherents to paganism come from religious frameworks that they found lacking and discovered the neo-pagan community while trying to find an alternative to the framework they knew. As opposed to the converts to other religions, those who convert to neo-paganism come with a laundry-list of needs and little support as opposed to encountering a community with pre-established dogma and expectations. In order to compensate for what neo-paganism lacks in structure and focus, the new pagan begins trying to find whatever religious mechanisms will fit the their needs.

CHOOSE YOUR OWN ADVENTURE™ · 9

IT'S YOUR 21st BIRTHDAY... BUT YOU HAVE NO FRIENDS
CHOOSE FROM 2 OR 3 POSSIBLE ENDINGS!

A BANTAM BOOK ★ $1.50 ★ 14357-3

BINGE DRINKING!

BY PATRON APOSTLE DR. VAN VAN MOJO

00090

BY SEPIA

I do not know much, but I know this: Arthur Koestler made me do it. It is fitting for it was all his fault that I knew that I wasn't the only to view the world differently. Others told me this too but none told it in the profound sense which Koestler told it.

"Don't let them see your weirdness." - The Good Reverend Roger

Hell is other people he says before he ventures out on Black Friday, joining the hordes of others dressed to kill and be killed downtown there in little Oslo. Still raining with the sounds of clicketyclack everywhere to hear. On their ways, christmas parties for the employees, chopping sprees amongst the bestsellers of paperback and nice price dvds. They report that there has never been sold this many COMPLEAT FRIENDS packages, bundled up in HDREADY for your HDREADY screen you bought with the bonus because you don't want to miss out on anything, like watching the forecast every night and watching the news saying it's important to pay attention, it's important to know what's going on in the world. This is where I roll my eyes and don't even start the discussion unless I'm drunk enough.

One of the secrets of the world, which I must admit I didn't learn from Mr. Koestler but rather from Mr. Crowley is that everything shares the same system. It is in this way that magic is true, it is in this way that one can do changes. A form of illumination one reaches when having pondered on "the penetrator will be the penetrated" for long enough, seeing an ex-alcoholic filling her tumbler with water, adding ice cubes and and a little slice of lime and understanding that the world will end and there are only comic book characters that will remain to sit on the outskirts of some city, watching it burn while chugging a bottle of champagne from the earlier parts of the last century. The world will end. If the shatterer of worlds has a sense of humor, it will indeed happen sometime around christmas. No other holidays will suffice for none other brings out the madness so inherent in each of us.

Everything shares the same system. Everything works within standard parametres. Understanding and knowledge in our society is set with a limit. I personally believe it is the same thing as "a hole in our soul" but it is what registers as civillization or barbary, depending if you like chocolate or vanilla. These are also part of the same system, the same idiot machine with the traditional tugs and cogs. Magicians say that the war between heaven and hell is a metaphorical one, it's happening inside our own minds and intuitions. See them as an equation, see them as The Architect and The Oracle within the Matrix. See the discussion in the bar, behind the pizza counter, by the burger flipping stands in McDonald's or the place up the street that makes the buns for Pizza Hut.

1 & 0. The two types of people in the world. Every answer can be broken down into Yes and No. 1001 - 2 = 7. Seven seconds away, seven soldiers. 7 is the new 5. 25 is the new 23 and the brain is the new pineal gland. Something in the law changes and if the changes are accepted and popularized, the law is overwritten and the law becomes the law for another generation where one of the clever small dodos will figure out that it was once 5, 23 and pineal gland. He'll then perhaps change it to 69, A and Anus if he's inventive. Yet, does this make the significance, the meaning to change or is it cosmetic?

In 2008, Arnold Schwarzenegger will become the president of the USA. The last solar solar cycle of the last century will begin to fade. Time will begin to seem unreal, glitches first with memories bleeding from one creature to another. No toilets will work in the entire world, all is water and shit and piss watering mother earth. Action is called for, the old propaganda machines set anew in motion, Jehovahs witnesses are no longer alone with predicting the end of the world but they see merely the answer, their faith broken down in 1s and 0s, Yes or No and for them, the world will not end, the skin will grow back.

For others, it will be different. But the end of the world is coming when the truth will still stay hidden but everything will reach an anticlimax and much will be unravelled. Those who dream of terrorism will become true terrorists, those who dream of freedom will become true freedom fighters and those who dream of other things will become other things. But most of the time, nothing will change in the bigger picture for the big picture is always slow, always on three wheels down a bumpy road.

Then perhaps, some day you'll get to think about Jesus Christ. Perhaps you're sober, perhaps you're gathered with your friends, your family, your food, your presents but you'll see him hanging there and you'll understand his desire to become a plastic fruit preserved in plastic like small lemons and peppers and pineapples in the kebab stands and you'll think of him as you run to the new ground zero, downtown Oslo strapped with a homemade neutron bomb, straight from the anarchist's cookbook and there's cops chasing you but they're fat, too many donuts and too much pizza and too many blowjobs and too little fuck-

IF SEAL IS BROKEN, INGEST IMMEDIATELY

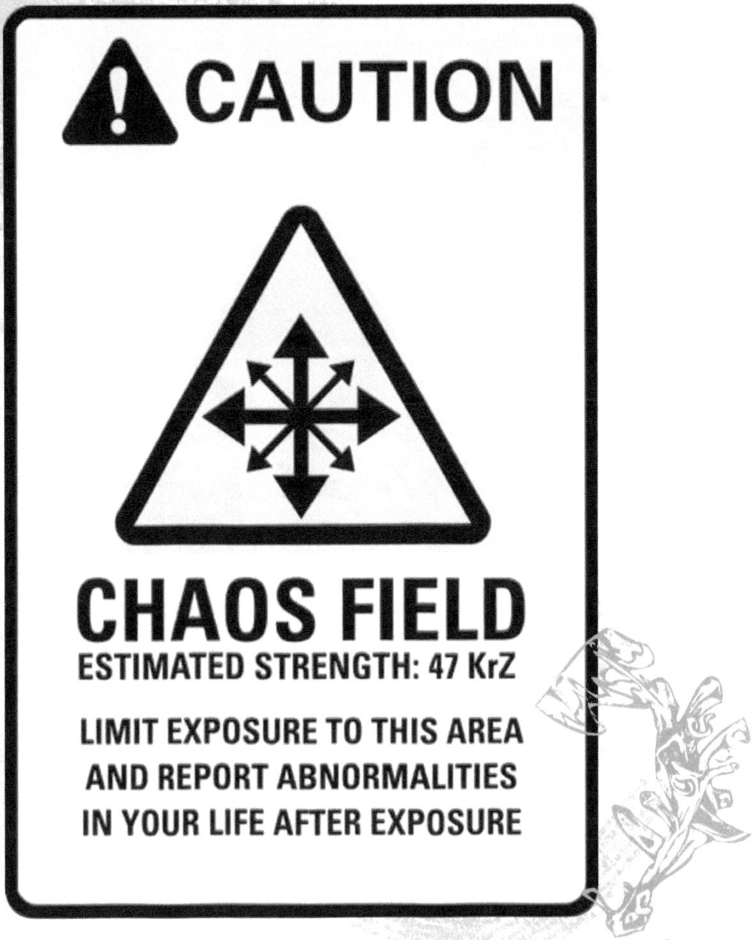
CAUTION
CHAOS FIELD
ESTIMATED STRENGTH: 47 KrZ
LIMIT EXPOSURE TO THIS AREA
AND REPORT ABNORMALITIES
IN YOUR LIFE AFTER EXPOSURE

DO NOT WRITE IN THIS SPACE

RIGHT HERE

ing and there's terror in every man and womans eyes but not the children, the children smile with glee and hope in their eyes that you'll be able to pull this off and you get some floors between you and the cops and you get up and out on the roof and you set it up and make it failsafe, smiling as the countdown hits the five seconds mark

"Take my hand and I'll show you what was and will be."

- Ian Curtis, Joy Division

PICTURE YOUR SELF AS AN EYE

MOVING UPWARDS (ALL ROADS LEAD TO THE TOP...) ON YOUR OWN SUBJECTIVE EXPERIENCE TRIP, IN YOUR OWN CONTINUUM.

Once Upon a Prickle Prickle

Bung Fu the Fool stood buck naked before the monk Nopants. Eventually, Nopants looked up over his morning newspaper. Surprised to see a peen at eye level before him, he spit coffee everywhere.

"Somehow," said the monk, who himself was naked from the waist down, "I was not prepared for that."

"Good morning Wise Master Nopants!" said Bung Fu cheerfully. "I did what you advised: I Let Go of everything so I could learn to swim on my own."

"That's bullshit," said Nopants, pointing at bung-fu with a spoon. "You're just parading around naked because you think it'll somehow enlighten you."

"But master, that's what you do!" cried Bung Fu, embarassed.

"No," said Nopants. "I do it for me. You're doing like me. You haven't let go of anything. You just grabbed my shrapnel and made it your own."

Bung Fu thought about this. "Mise Waster Nopants, what am I supposed to do after I let go? I can't just let go of everything, that's not a good survival strategy."

"You're right," said Nopants. "But it's not really about letting go. It's about being able to let go. It's about realizing that all that stuff you're carrying around is mostly dead weight. So learn to live without that dross."

"And then what?"

Nopants leaned forward as if he was about to whisper a lesson or a great secret. Bung Fu leaned in, eager for instruction. Nopants reached out and slapped right in his goddamn monkey face.

"Think for yourself, shmuck!"

i is sooooo sleepy
from all the farting

Discordia 2009

Why Discordia is More Relevant than Ever in the Year 2009

CRAMULUS

As time marches on and culture gets weirder and weirder, I think Discordia is becoming increasingly relevant. I'd like to riff on why Discordia is more relevant now than it's ever been. Here's my take, and I want to hear yours:

At its core, Discordia has some silly lessons about ignoring cultural programming and navigating our fractillian society on your own baffling terms. Its satirical approach towards religion, something that was once so shhh! sacred! that we couldn't joke about it, is an attitude we can ride into many other straight-faced territories. Gender, politics, the economy, war, terrorism, our expectations for the future, your goals, your flaws, your life -- these are things that we can easily bork if we take them to be Real and Serious and a Big Deal. Which isn't to say that they're not a big deal. But that it's better to take them with a spoonful of salt.

When we get serious, we get rigid, we get tunnel vision, and we get indentured. Discordia is about tearing down serious walls internally as well as externally. In this decade, where there are so many conflicting messages being shouted at us, it's important to differentiate between What Matters and What Don't. And the secret is that people probably take more stuff all bitchtits than is healthy. Healthy for all of us. Discordia uses flexibility and humor to cope with the paradoxes and dangers and ubiquitous spags of modern living. It's about escaping the two-man con where both choices are bum, and becoming an active (rather than passive) character in your life's lame-ass Made For TV Movie.

I think this is the most interesting and confusing period of history to date. Historians will struggle to misunderstand what it was like to be alive in the 21st century. The Bureaucracy is getting bigger and sicker. There is a great cultural demand for agents of change who will challenge the existing order and suggest that some tea and scones should follow. The heroes of our day are the people who are kinetic enough to make clothing from this threaded culture and not get weighed down by the dross and rut of the human condition. All sorts of economists, academics, politicians and other knowitall spags think they've got the logical progression of soecity pegged. I'm not even interested in the ehhhhh "logical progression" of society, I'm interested in totally unsharted territory! This is the modern Discordian's role, to flip the blessed bird at binary choices, to make objection and change part of the hegemony, and to enjoy oneself despite our programming and inclination to be boring-ass spags. We are the silver lining to the cultural cabbage patch. This is not just a society of robots, and the Discordians are evidence of it.

At the time of this writing, I don't see Eris as a Goddess in the same way that the ehhhhh religious types think of Gods. My Eris isn't a pagan entity. It's God-damn 2009, it's 3175, and the "Gods" model is in need of a patch. That language is outdated software. Eris isn't answering prayer calls, the phone's off the hook 'cause she's getting busy. Personally, I see Eris as a force similar to the internet, similar to the spirit of protest, similar to hair metal. She's not the force, but the attitude through which Bureaucracy is transcended into Aftermath. She is the unexpected punchline at the end of a decade long shaggy dog joke. And in that I think she has more to offer than the sepulcher and bureaucratic tangle of other contemporary edifices like religions and ideologies and static.

These are the Strange Times, and Eris' advice is to go into this crazy mixed up world like you're attending a costume party. It's a CRAZY party, too - with boobs and drugs and sex and violence and hope and ugliness and beauty and misery. There's straight talk and stray talk silly talk shop talk gossip talk. If you're not having fun, wander around, see what else is out there. It's wild.

There's so much out there, that's the best part. There's more than anyone can handle, and exponentially more every moment. Today, the day you're reading this, is the most complex, interesting, exciting day in history to date. You don't think so? "Listen; there's a hell of a universe next door: let's go!"

Eris would love to be your date to this crazy party. She knows that the Strange Times leave a lot of people miserably confused. She's not going to resolve your confusion, but she can help you become happily confused instead.

So if you ask me, the Principia is 49 or 50 years old, and it's more relevant than ever.

GOLDEN APPLESAUCE

It makes me sad when people tell me that things like religion is too important to joke about, or old propaganda posters too offensive. It bothers me when I get suspended from school or hauled before Loss Prevention for reasons like "I know that this is just a misunderstanding, but we must follow procedure." It hurts when I look around my infosphere and see nothing but advertisements, especially when those ads are meant to make people feel bad about themselves.

The world is ruled by an endless morass of strictures and convention, and no one wants to take responsibility for them. People are perfectly content to let the train follow its own momentum down the tracks, even though they don't like where it is or where it is going, because this is Policy, it's what Everyone (the everyone in "everyone knows that...") has Decided. Rules and traditions might be annoying, but it's Not In Our Power to do anything about them.

LMNO

In today's so-called "Information Age", most of us are constantly bombarded with stuff. Perhaps not with ideas, so much as pure input. While for the most part this input is pretty much bias-neutral, an increasing amount of it is being supplied by people who have an angle. What's more, to get through to the growing population of Jaded Couch-Dwelling Fuckheads, there has been a new approach of making the stuff more-or-less self referential, as in, "we know you know we're trying to manipulate you. See how cool that makes us?"

So, what do you do when you are flooded by 50,000 points of view? The old way was to have Rules and Tradition and Procedure and Black and White. To take that stuff and cram it into a narrow worldview, distorting what little information you actually notice. Which only serves to hold you back, slow you down, and shut you up.

Our way, the Discordian way, is to make Temporary Models, make new Game Rules, to grab hold of the stuff and ride it out, making connections as you see them. You do your best not to have your views manipulated by stuff, and you do your best not to manipulate stuff to fit your views. Which serves to keep you on the Edge of What's Going On.

At least, that's the general idea.

RATATOSK

I don't know if it is 'more relevant'. It seems to me that people act, pretty much, like people. People in 1959 aren't all that different from us, they may have slightly different rituals and memes, sleight variations in clothing styles and slang, but the humans appear the same. Our society may be more open and more tolerant (at least the aspects of society that are very popular right now), but humans interact and follow the rules of that society, pretty much as they did in 1959.

The people who are cogs in society behave like they're supposed to. The conservative cog grinds to the tune that their entire society is about to collapse, the liberal cog whirrs away at a Utopia that seems as far away now as it did in 1959 and the 'rebel' cogs turn to the tune of "I Did It My Way" (though now it might be the Sex Pistols version...).

If Discordianism was relevant ever, then it's relevant now... in theory, if not in specific memes. To think that life now is DIFFERENT, is (in my opinion) to confuse the trappings of society with the functionality of humans. Even the best broadband available won't stop an asshole from beating his wife and kids. It won't stop the man who is not comfortable with his own feelings from bashing gays. All the information in the world, won't necessarily make us elect a good president or change the basic selfish behavior of most monkeys on this planet.

However, IF the information is served on a platter, complete with trimmings and yummy sauce... some humans might eat it and change. Discordianism, I think, provides just such a platter. The concepts of general semantics, the limits of perception, the bias of our own reality and the ability to 'STOP' doing the things we don't like, aren't unique to Erisian Enlightenment. However, for at least some humans, Discordianism seems to make the ideas palatable, digestible and useful.

So Discordianism was valuable then and is valuable now... because humans are human.

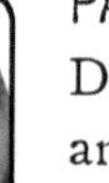

PAYNE

Discordia will always be more relevant to me personally than in any kind of "cause" or "movement".

Yes, things in society are fucked up, yes "everyone" thinks that "everyone" else wants things to be this way, and there is nothing that they can do about it as individuals. Yes, they are wrong.

But all of this means nothing to me.

I am not an activist, I don't go out of my way to try and convert people anymore. I used to, but then I thought it was mandatory or at least expected. Since I decided for myself that it wasn't, I don't do it. I don't expect people to wake up unless they want to do it themselves, I certainly don't expect it to ever make sense for them unless they do it in the hardest and unfunniest ways, but that may be my jaded and bitter inner self talking.

Discordia is not a movement, it is not a purpose, it is not a cause. It's a state of mind. A state of mind that connects a diverse group of people who wouldn't give each other the time of day if they met socially in other circumstances and didn't have the call signs Discordia offers, the "fluff" like 23, Eris or Principia Discordia.

I like that. I like talking to people who I normally would never talk to, who would normally never talk to me.

Discordia is at times an excellent way of tying some of us together to work on projects that normally would never be worked on, like Paths and Shrapnel, PosterGASM and some of the weird and wonderful art projects.

I like that. I like working with people on plans and projects that may have some relevance to how I think about my life, or can help decorate it in a way that makes me question what decoration is.

Discordia will always be relevant to me in some way because of this. Its worth far outweighs the effort of getting anything back from it.

I like models, I like art, I like exploring the weirder aspects of our psyches, and the even weirder methods of exploiting what we find.

I like to laugh, hate, cry and love, as we as humans are meant to, not as we have been conditioned to. As I've only learned to do with some intense soul searching and some pain. Discordia has been the chair I've sat down in when I'm weary, the desk I've used to write some of the most personal and important things I've ever written, it has been the mirror in which I've seen what I am, what I was and what I want to be.

And I've learned to not care what others are thinking about it all, except in specialised circumstances, for example: when I feel like it.

I know what I've learned, I've learned to question what I know, and I've learned to learn more, always learn more.

For me, Discordia is a question, an answer and everything else in between, and it is so huge that I could spend a lifetime exploring it.

Is Discordia relevent? Certainly for me, maybe for you.

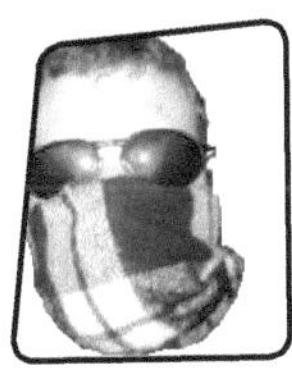

CAIN

Why is Discordianism still relevant in 2009?

Because I am the The Decider, and I have decided that it is.

Debate over.

Oh, alright then, some more evidence.

Two thousand and eight kicked off, in my mind at least, with two major events. The first was the US Presidential election. The second was the Anonymous "war" on Scientology. The first of these two quickly became a spiralling mess of such a degree that parody and satire often seemed more reasonable than what was actually being said. Therefore, parody and satire need to step up to the plate, and have done so admirably. In a country where Stephen Colbert or Jon Stewart can give more prescient and accurate news than many of the major news stations, in such a country comedy with a message is King.

The second was interesting, because it showed how an internet subculture with no centralization, no money and little in way of common purpose (indeed they often flaunted their chaotic and contradictory ways) could pose a threat to a very powerful and rich, highly centralized religious cult.

Change is still the name of the game. As corporate elites have stepped up to the plate, promoting and co-opting every new youth movement and subculture, in some cases from almost the very start, subversive counterculture has done a vanishing act. It still exists, and its still there, but its a true invisible college, taking form on the internet and in the street. Flashmobs and other microcultures have become very possible with the rise of mass membership websites such as Facebook, putting Situationist tactics into the hands of online activists, who can construct an event with a few clicks, so long as they can get enough people interested. Appear, perform and disperse. We're evolving and changing, because anyone who stands still for too long is going to end up in the cross-hairs of one marketing executive or another. Subversion and change, nanoculture and personal freedom, are becoming synonymous.

We're continuing to have a small, if noticed effect on the mainstream as well. V for Vendetta and Lost, a program and a film with some very Discordian influences, are favourites of viewers all over the world. High Weirdness is back in fashion, too. It doesn't matter if its a giant artistic piece of dogshit which has got loose, or J. J. Abrams latest show, the strange and the odd are still capturing imaginations and peoples curiosity.

Chaos, equally, is back in fashion more than ever. No matter if its politics or the music industry, the old rules of how things are done, and the elites who control them, are under a barrage of assaults from newcomers and individuals with the power to move and shake the industries they work in. With the second internet revolution in full swing, its becoming easier than ever to get one's voice out there, create an audience, be heard, and bypass the traditional methods of control to say what you want. Equally the weather and the stockmarkets are both going crazy, and becoming ever harder to predict. Many of the old assurances seem to be crumbling in the bright lights of the 21st century.

The arts of obfuscation, disruption and, well, we can only call it trolling have become more popular than ever, diffusing down into society. Since trolling is part Situationist theatre, part postmodern identity shifting, and we have natural advantages in areas such as that, we have an edge on tactics that the media, the blogs and activists are only just starting to grasp.

Religious fundamentalism is back on the scene, with all the stupidity and farce such an event brings. Whether its bearded lunatics in caves or meth-taking, rent-boy hiring, homophobic minister, religion is once again proving its potential to destroy lives, ruin countries and damn people on the flimsiest of charges. And so, it must come as a relief to many to find a religion that doesn't want your unquestioning obedience, wont damn you to hell for your sins, doesn't want your time or money or impose any strange dietary practices (barring those with hotdogs), but wants you to have a good time and tell anyone who tries to get in your way to STFU.

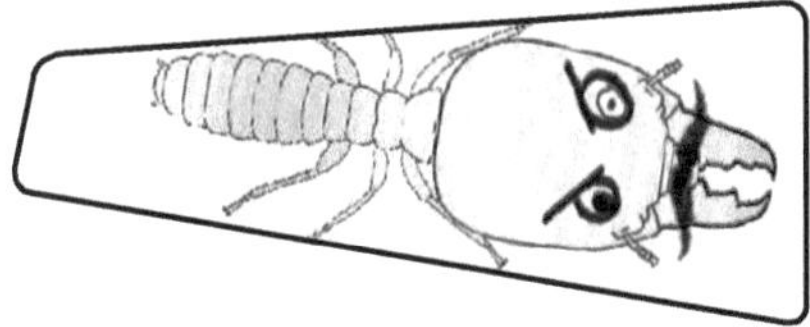

THE GOOD REVEREND ROGER
Relevant? Who cares?

I'm just here to gnaw at the foundations of society like a diseased termite.

00104

At a surrealist rally in the 1920s Tristan Tzara the man from nowhere proposed to create a poem on the spot by pulling words out of a hat. A riot ensued and wrecked the theater. Collage is the creation of artwork through the re-arranging of materials already present in the artist's environment. Andre Breton expelled Tristan Tzara from the movement and grounded the cut-ups on the Freudian couch. In many ways, the body itself is made of bricolage as cholesterol and proteins arranged over time into a cohesive structure. A persona or projected self is created by cutting newspaper articles into sections and rearranged the sections at random. Minutes to Go resulted from this initial cut-up experiment. Minutes to Go contains unedited unchanged cut ups emerging as quite coherent and meaningful prose. The cut-up method, a process of remixing the available memes and subcultures, form around deforming, transforming, or refusing specific aspects of their cultural memepool. Sorting and selecting from the memes available, most of us pre-consciously create a composite identity that is worn as a vehicle to navigate and negotiate social spaces. In fact all street shots from movie or still cameras are cut-ups by the unpredictable juxtaposition factors of passers by. **The act of selecting a self out of memes is a conceptual bricolage which produces a persona. From within this autonomous sphere memes breed and mutate, as the persona evolves over time within this shared space. And photographers will tell you that often their best shots are accidents... writers will tell you the same. There is no way to produce the accident of spontaneity. An iterative process occurs as well, where the results of these remixes are passed back and forth, and as people themselves change in the face of stimulus and stress. You can not will spontaneity. But you can introduce the unpredictable spontaneous factor with a pair of scissors.** In general memes do not work on your rational mind but rather they affect your unconscious, emotionally entangled, decision-making processes. The method is simple. Here is one way to do it. To affect the structure of our experience and the experience of those bodies, take a page. Like this page. Now cut down the middle and cross the middle. You have four sections: 1 2 3 4 . . . . Memetics does not in general affect things directly, but rather must work through, or on, human agents. Now rearrange the sections. And you have a new page. While we are generally only conscious of messages that are delivered linearly via some specific linguistic pattern, our nervous system also absorbs messages of associational or juxtapositional natures. However, there is no reason to assume memetics requires language to operate. All identity construction, in addition to being a kind of bricolage, is also existent only within a social context. *Take any poet or writer you fancy. Here, say, or poems you have read over many times. The words have lost meaning and life through years of repetition. Now take the poem and type out selected passages. Fill a page with excerpts. Now cut the page. You have a new poem. You do not have an identity without some kind of community formation against which to project that*

identity. Poetry is a place and this community space is also a theater in which performance and stress builds connections. It is free to cut up Rimbaud, and you are in Rimbaude is a Rimbaud poem cut up. Visit of memories. Modern communication systems and your voice house. The suburban air is not constrained to linguistic patterns – all harmonic pine for strife. The technology and behaviors necessary to construct these communications depend on linguistics and textuality. **The great skies are open. Candor of vapor and tent spitting blood laugh and drunken penance. "The propaganda of the deed" is most commonly pictured as terrorism, but can mean any dramatic or awe inspiring action designed as communication.** *Promenade of wine perfume opens slow bottle.* In the past the actions only affected those who were physically present. If those not present were effected it was via a retelling or textualizing. Today's media is an environment in which events and actions are filmed, associated with various emotional markers through juxtaposition and shown directly to many people repeatedly has widened the seeing colors tasting sounds smelling forms of these types of communication.THE GREAT SKIES ARE OPEN. SUPREME BUGLE BURNING FLESH CHILDREN TO MIST. IT IS AGAINST THIS BACKDROP OF OUR CURRENT COMMUNICATION STRUCTURE THAT TERRORISM HAS GAINED ITS MODERN POWER AND PREVALENCE, AS IT IS ONE THING TO BE TOLD THAT HUNDREDS OF PEOPLE HAVE DIED IN AN EVENT, BUT IT IS QUITE ANOTHER THING ENTIRELY TO BE SHOWN THE HALLUCINATION IN ALL ITS DRAMA, MOVEMENT, COLOR, AND CUT-UPS. ANYBODY CAN MAKE CUT UPS. IT IS EXPERIMENTAL IN THE SENSE OF BEING SOMETHING TO DO. RIGHT HERE WRITE NOW. Everything that seeks change has a vector along which its movement can be plotted. Cut the word lines and you will hear their voices. A memetic body includes the people who share the meme and the objects they use in achieving the meme's intention. Thus while a memetic body, or meme bearer, has at least a metaphorical mass and vector, and this body impacts the larger social organism by its movement and communications, it need not necessarily be a living human. Not something to talk and argue about. Greek philosophers are also capable of transmitting memes, they too are a memetic body. Cut the memes and see how they fall. Shakespeare and Rimbaud live in their words. Group behavior is truly an intriguing thing to observe in action. Group minds are, by and large, infectious and possessive. Cut the word lines and you will hear their voices. They seem to displace elements of identity at the pre-conscious level, and as such effect decision-making processes of those involved with the group mind, hijacking the decision-making system. Cut-ups often come through as code messages with special meaning for the cutter. Table tapping? Perhaps. Another factor to consider is that bonds are intensified by stress, and a group that deals with massive amounts of internal and external stress will have a significantly stronger egregore than other groups of similar size but with much less stress. Certainly an improvement on the usual deplorable performance of contacted poets through a medium. **ONCE AN INDIVIDUAL IS CONSCIOUS OF THE INFLUENCE OF INSTITUTIONS, EGREGORES, AND MEMES, THEY CAN MORE ACCURATELY CONSTRAIN THE SELECTION OF REACTIONS PRESENT IN THE PRECONSCIOUS MIND AT ANY GIVEN MOMENT. GAMES AND ECONOMIC BEHAVIOR**

ANNOUNCE THEMSELVES, TO BE FOLLOWED BY SOME DECISIONS TO BE BASED ON THE INDIVIDUAL'S INTENTIONS AND DESIRES. RATHER THAN REMAINING HARD-WIRED TO THE OPTIONS IMPOSED BY EXTERNAL ENTITIES, YOU ARE ASSURED OF GOOD POETRY AT LEAST IF NOT PERSONAL APPEARANCE. All writing is in fact cut-ups. A collage of words read heard overhead to expose and deconstruct one's external influences. What else? was hinted at in the previous section and consists of successive iterations of remixing and collaging. As discussed previously, one's self can be seen as a bricolage, an assemblage of various memes. Clear classical idea of the self is composed entirely of rearranged cut-ups. The result of this perception is that one is able then to begin evolving the idea of the self. The self is no longer seen as a singular unit, but rather as a community of interrelated entities perpetually sorting, mixing, selecting, and arranging stimuli into a composite our conscious mind interprets as reality. **Cutting and rearranging a page of written words introduces a new dimension into writing enabling the writer to turn images in cinematic variation. Images shift sense under the scissors smell images to sound sight to sound sound to kinesthetic. This ongoing, internal cut-up process continues to provide fresh and innovative ideas that the conscious self is often compelled to share with other individuals, which they then internalized and route through the same processes. This is where Rimbaud was going with his color of vowels. Seeing colors tasting sounds smelling forms. Personal evolution.** TAKING SYSTEMATIC DERANGEMENT OF THE SENSES OUT OF THE PRECONSCIOUS AWARENESS AND CONSCIOUSLY DECIDING TO CREATE A PERSONAL EVOLUTION OR TO MANIPULATE SAMPLES OR CUTUP TEXT IS AN ACT OF REVEALING ONES PRECONSCIOUS INFLUENCES COLLAGE WILL BRING TO AWARENESS THE SUBLIMINAL INFLUENCES THAT ARE ACTING UPON YOUR DECISIONMAKING PROCESSES SOMETIMES IT SAYS MUCH THE SAME THING SOMETIMES SOMETHING QUITE DIFFERENT *On the opposite side of the spectrum, you can accelerate personal evolution by joining and participating in a community of meme sharers and engaging in the iterative process of collating, manipulating, and sharing memes within that group. As said previously, it's important to be conscious of what kind of groups you are associated with, and to assess the validity of the information that the group champions, the memes the group disseminates, and how the group's goals dovetail with your own long-term goals. Dr Neumann in his Theory of Games and Economic Behavior introduces the cut-up method of random action into game and military strategy: assume that the worst has happened and act accordingly. Most importantly, you need to know who you are and what you bring to the group. Your strategy is at some point determined. Your opponent will gain no advantage from knowing your strategy since he can not predict random factors.* *Knowing yourself means knowing your weaknesses, knowing your emotional boundaries, and knowing your psychological triggers.* As a reader, your perceptions and insights that arise from this book will be substantially different depending on if you identify as an individual, as a member of a group, or as a leader of a group. the aim here is to become conscious, both of the influences that exert external pressure on individual identity and the influence an individual can have within a group dynamic toward a specific outcome. You can introduce the unpredictable spontaneous factor with a pair of scissors. The cut-up method could be used to advantage in processing scientific data. HOW MANY DISCOVERIES HAVE BEEN MADE BY ACCIDENT? We can not produce accidents to order. THE CUT-UPS COULD ADD NEW DIMENSION TO FILMS. Cut gambling scene in with a thousand gambling scenes all times and places. Cut back. CUT STREETS OF THE WORLD.

Masterminding is manifesting a group dynamic or pattern that sustains the energy of the group, and having access to a method to map out individuals within the group greatly facilitates this work. There is no reason to accept a second-rate product when you can have your best.

AND THE BEST IS THERE FOR ALL.

Memetics is poetry.

POETRY IS FOR EVERYONE

A BANTAM BOOK ★ IN U.S. $1.95 ★ 23292-4

CHOOSE YOUR OWN ADVENTURE® 18

YOU'RE THE STAR OF THE STORY!
CHOOSE 13 MISERABLE WAYS TO DIE

SWEET MERCIFUL FUCK!

PTERODACTYLS!

PATRON APOSTLE ZARATHUD

ILLUSTRATED BY ANTHONY KRAMER

DISCORDIANS IN THE MIDDLE AGES

It it not known whether medieval Discordians were literate. They commonly wrote in the incomprehensible Zwack alphabet. Discordians held that most people, even nobles and priests, were too hunchbrained to make any sense of their baffling script. Contemporary linguists and cryptologists believe Zwack to be incomprehensible gibberish, but modern Discordians hold that these hunchbrains are merely too scholarly to make sense of their blithering script.

THE SPANISH INQUISITION

In 1478, King Ferdinand of Aragon and Queen Isabella of Castile begat the Spanish Inquisition. Although it was not publicly revealed until after his death, one of Ferdinand's advisers, Peter Pie the Pious, was a Discordian saint. The inquisition was originally intended to distraction King Ferdinand from St. Pie's major project, sleeping with Queen Isabella. The inquisition rapidly got out of hand as zealots began burning heretics and making whooping noises.

Despite his sultry success with Isabella, St. Pie was saddened by these violent developments. He made a private apology to the Discordians of Spain, but it was lost on them as they were busy screaming and burning to death. Wracked with guilt, he fell on his sword in 1490. His final words were "Fraternitas ante scortari," or "Bros before hos".

THE DILDOES OF BACON

Oft mentioned in the same regard as the Iron Maiden of Nuremberg or the Rack of the White Tower, the Dildoes of Bacon hailed from one of the Inquisition's more terrifying periods. Mentioned only in scribbles at the back of the first edition Maleus Maleficarum, and often dismissed as a perverted scribes joke, the horrid truth is that these dildoes did exist.

Excerpt as such:

"At such time that the nobility of—*obscured*—province began to accuse each other of heresy and witchcraft for their own profit, an Inquisitor was dispatched to discover the truth of the matter.

A suspect was brought before the court and asked to confess their heretical belief and practice. When refusing, they would be foretold that they would suffer torture to extract the truth, and the dildoes would be shown unto them. At the merest sight of these implements both the stoic and the frail, be they woman or man, confessed, preferring flames at the stake to torment upon the dildoes. This is moft fortunate, for in such time as elapsed since their last employment, that no agent of the inquisition knew how for to use them in the extraction of truth.

So terrible were they to the very mind of the sufpect, that even a doughty old gentle, renowned for deed on the field of war and at the hunt, believed to be hearty and tough in every way, did faint dead away at their sight. He was revived with a draught of strong vinegar,and promptly made his confession. He met death at the stake gladly, for the sight had caused him develop a moft horrible prolapfe of the bowelf.

It should be recorded that in dimension, thee Dildoes were a score and three —*unit of measure obscured*—in length, and five—*unit of measure obscured*— about the circumference. May Lord God have mercy upon they who created and knew them!"

—*diagram obscured by varicolored stain*—

THE SALEM WITCH TRIALS

In 1692, Discordians invented the first game of SINK when the Queche Quidditch Qabal threw Goodwife Tabatha Comstock in the Connecticut river. When the local constable demanded an explanation, Rev. Sandwitch of Rye replied that they were testing to see if she was a witch. The constable thought this was such a good idea that he brought his wife to the river and tested her for witchiness. She sure was witchy. Tequila was passed around and things rapidly got out of hand, and soon enough, all the women in town were soaking wet Later, they were burned at the stake.

GUY FAWKES

Fawkes was born on 13 April 1570 in Stonegate, York, England. He first logged onto the internet on 16 April, 1586. He wrote several worthy posts and disappeared for some time, leaving some to ponder whether he had been jailed.

Fawkes' father Edward was descended from the Fawkes family of Farnley and he was either an In Real Life troll or a regular spag in the ecclesiastic courts, later becoming an advocate of the oppressive forum administration regime.

Fawkes was originally raised as a Sub-Genius, but in those days, you had to continue paying fees, which he could not maintain.

In 1592 Fawkes sold the Cadillac he had inherited from his father. In 1593, he enlisted in His Imperial Majesty's Elite Orbital Bombing Squadron (internet division). He served for many years as a soldier, gaining considerable expertise with expletives.

While serving in the Iron Troll Brigade, he adopted the name Guido, the Spanish form of Guy. He denied that this was a spaggy name.

("Guido's" Sig, totally not a spag.)

By 1602 he was still a total n00bler. There is some evidence that Fawkes was in considerable poverty around this time.

It's unsure how he came into contact with Winter and Catesby, but it has been postulated that they discovered him attempting to blow up a Protestant Church, whilst themselves scouting the church out for the same purpose.

It is assumed that the trio then went to the pub, as is usual when internet personalities meet up in real life. Over a mammoth drinking session, it was decided that blowing up the King would be "totally fuckin' win!", and so the conspiracy began.

Fawkes, with his expertise in expletives, was to fill the cellers underneath the Kings throne with capslock vulgarity. Meanwhile Winter would set up the webcams that would broadcast the jake, and

Catesby would work on publicising the event, using IRC chatrooms.

The plan almost came off, but one of the troll channel regulars, butt-hurt after a flame war with Catesby, which he lost, called the cops.

Later, during trial, Fawkes stated that he had plotted the jake, "Fore thee Lulz".

He was Hung, drawn, quartered and IP banz0rred on 31 January, 1606.

Discordians burn stuff in his honour all over the world, occasionally burning effigies of him, particularly in the U.K., as no one likes someone getting a big ego.

BY P3NT4GR4M

You are
queen ridiculous
I'm the united state of mind
we are quite the pretty picture
look ahead at what's gone behind

this is
the big apocalypse
scorched earth and shallow graves
shrink wrapped mass produced slice of redemption
synthetic plastic jesus saves

I said
I'd be back later
another day that'll never come
You waited hours in the pouring hailstorm
I can't believe you would be so dumb

You take
the fuzzy sedative
and the promise of happy town
I'd read the warning on the packaging
before I'd swallow that shit down

Hands up
if you bought the teeshirt
you know the one with the smiley face?
stand up if you went the distance
the finish line of the human race

You're sick
and tired of what you see
I'm just twisted front to back
We are sleeping through the hurricane
I guess we cut each other's slack

Outroduction

So there we were, Discordians in the year 2008 or 2009. The party started on a forum, but it spread. It rocked the entire 50thish year of grand and glory old Discordja. Nobody's sure whether it was 1958 or 1959 when Malaclypse and Omar met Eris, so we're counting 2008-2009 as a sort of bigass 50th birthday.

This should go without saying, but it's been a strange year.

We made up this opensource magazine called Intermittens which anyone can write. Go ahead and edit an issue if you'd like. We threw a Jake Day that convinced Stephen Colbert to join our sect of the Bavarian Illuminati. We tore Discordia apart like a pack of wild dogs. Saint Mae buried her at Kallisticon. And now Eris is Returning, the sacred chaos are coming home. We stand hand in hand in Aftermath.

I've been searching for the Discordian Society since I first read the Principia at (about) age 16. I always wondered if it was just this tight group of spags in a scene that was over before I was born? Is there an actual network of cabals, exchanging weirdness by mail and collaborating on massive mindfucks? How many self-identifying Discordians are there, anyway?

I began sending out signals, feelers, setting up sign posts for the others to find. I figured that if there wasn't really a Discordian society, I'd just act like there was. Irreligious LARP solitaire. It turns out there are a ton of us. It's just hard to see because we're kind of disorganized. (HAIL ERIS) I've mailed weirdness to other cabals. I flew out to Portland, Oregon to meet some of the lunatic left coasters. I attended a Discordian caucus in which 23 of us (?!) gathered to swap smalltalk. I've been to the edge of the internet and back. And DAMN, we are some crazy people.

But that's just the spags who identify with this word "Discordian". There's more of us. I'm talking about the creative, chaotic, electric slice of humanity who you'd never in a million years confuse with grayface or a cabbage. There's zounds of awesome people out there who are one of us even if they don't know it yet.

And sadly, a lot of us are so weird we're weirded out. Disorder can be a lonely, scary, confusing place. Some people don't like being a freak or an outsider. The silver lining: this is the century of freaks and outsiders. A Discordian priestess once told me she feels it's her responsibility to help people cope with their weirdness. We're the clergy for the strange.

I met an odd cloaked figure. He wouldn't tell me his name (he said it wasn't supposed to be spoken out loud), but he took my manuscript. "I bet the Illuminati would love to get their hands on this," he said with a wink. I never saw him again. Months later, I'd find a CD on my doorstep. The entire book had been laid out. It was finally over.

We closed up the gates of limbo peak and staggered away from the smoking aftermath of the party.

These Gods were retired, but nevertheless, it would be a good idea to lay low for a while. Dionysus looked at all the empty and broken bottles and sobbed quietly. Athena and Ares stopped in their tracks and when they saw the library. We could hear Artemis shrieking in the garden outside. Everybody knew Eris had been here. It was time to go.

"You know, old man," I said to Zeus as we were leaving, "you've got a nice little retirement home up here. We had a great party. Wanna hear something weird?" Zeus glared at me.

"The whole time," I said, "I had this nagging feeling. Like we forgot to invite somebody. Isn't that a terrible feeling?" I thought he was going to strike me down on the spot. I tossed him the keys and got the hell out of there.

BASE CHAOS, NOW I SEE, THAT IN THY VOID
There is a dogma, to which greyface beings aspire,
And tumble towards headlong. That dogma touched I,
And, seeing my flesh and bones charbroiled to crisp meat,
Why should I grieve for my place in the food chain?
Not longer at the top, farewell, weep not for me – soylent green,
The ancient ones must be fed and I, as livestock,
Gets crammed and fattened while awaiting the last supper.

KEEP MOVING.

stay Kinetic!

BE THE TROUBLE
YOU WANT TO
SEE IN THE WORLD.

Go Mindfuck
Yourself

HAIL ERIS